Women with Disabilities: Found Voices

Women with Disabilities: Found Voices

Mary E. Willmuth, PhD
Lillian Holcomb, PhD

Editors

The Haworth Press, Inc.
New York • London • Norwood (Australia)

Women with Disabilities: Found Voices has also been published as *Women & Therapy*, Volume 14, Numbers 3/4 1993.

The development, preparation, and publication of this work has been undertaken with great care. However, the publisher, employees, editors, and agents of The Haworth Press and all imprints of The Haworth Press, Inc., including The Haworth Medical Press and Pharmaceutical Products Press, are not responsible for any errors contained herein or for consequences that may ensue from use of materials or information contained in this work. Opinions expressed by the author(s) are not necessarily those of The Haworth Press, Inc.

The Haworth Press, Inc., 10 Alice Street, Binghamton, NY 13904-1580 USA

Library of Congress Cataloging-in-Publication Data

Women with disabilities : found voices / Mary E. Willmuth, Lillian Holcomb, editors.
     p. cm.
     "Women with disabilities . . . has also been published as Women & therapy, volume 14, number 3/4, 1993"–T.p. verso.
     Includes bibliographical references.
     ISBN 1-56204-477-1 (acid-free paper). – ISBN 1-56023-046-0 (hpp: acid-free paper)
    1. Handicapped women–United States. 2. Handicapped women–United States–Social conditions. 3. Handicapped women–Psychology. I. Willmuth, Mary E. II. Holcomb, Lillian.
HV1569.3.W65W665 1993
362.4'082–dc20   93-30402
                                                                CIP

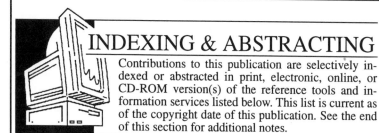

INDEXING & ABSTRACTING

Contributions to this publication are selectively indexed or abstracted in print, electronic, online, or CD-ROM version(s) of the reference tools and information services listed below. This list is current as of the copyright date of this publication. See the end of this section for additional notes.

- *Abstracts of Research in Pastoral Care & Counseling*, Loyola College, 7135 Minstrel Way, Suite 101, Columbia, MD 21045

- *Academic Index (on-line)*, Information Access Company, 362 Lakeside Drive, Foster City, CA 94404

- *Alternative Press Index*, Alternative Press Center, Inc., P.O. Box 33109, Baltimore, MD 21218

- *Bulletin Signaletique*, INIST/CNRS-Service Gestion des Documents Primaires, 2, allee du Parc de Brabois, F-54514 Vandoeuvre-les-Nancy, Cedex, France

- *Digest of Neurology and Psychiatry*, The Institute of Living, 400 Washington Street, Hartford, CT 06106

- *Expanded Academic Index,* Information Access Company, 362 Lakeside Drive, Forest City, CA 94404

- *Family Violence & Sexual Assault Bulletin*, Family Violence & Sexual Assault Institute, 1310 Clinic Drive, Tyler, TX 75701

- *Feminist Periodicals: A Current Listing of Contents*, Women's Studies Librarian-at-Large, 728 State Street, 430 Memorial Library, Madison, WI 53706

- *Higher Education Abstracts*, Claremont Graduate School, 740 North College Avenue, Claremont, CA 91711

(continued)

- *Index to Periodical Articles Related to Law*, University of Texas, 727 East 26th Street, Austin, TX 78705

- *Inventory of Marriage and Family Literature (online and hard copy)*, National Council on Family Relations, 3989 Central Avenue NE, Suite 550, Minneapolis, MN 55421

- *Mental Health Abstracts (online through DIALOG)*, IFI/Plenum Data Company, 3202 Kirkwood Highway, Wilmington, DE 19808

- *Periodical Abstracts, Research 1*, UMI Data Courier, P.O. Box 32770, Louisville, KY 40232-2770

- *Periodical Abstracts, Research 2*, UMI Data Courier, P.O. Box 32770, Louisville, KY 40232-2770

- *Psychological Abstracts (PsycINFO)*, American Psychological Association, P.O. Box 91600, Washington, DC 20090-1600

- *Sage Family Studies Abstracts*, Sage Publications, Inc., 2455 Teller Road, Newbury Park, CA 91320

- *Social Work Research & Abstracts*, National Association of Social Workers, 750 First Street NW, 8th Floor, Washington, DC 20002

- *Studies on Women Abstracts*, Carfax Publishing Company, P.O. Box 25, Abingdon, Oxfordshire OX14 3UE, United Kingdom

- *Women Studies Abstracts*, Rush Publishing Company, P.O. Box 1, Rush, NY 14543

- *Women's Studies Index (indexed comprehensively)*, G.K. Hall & Co., 866 Third Avenue, New York, NY 10022

(continued)

SPECIAL BIBLIOGRAPHIC NOTES

related to indexing, abstracting, and library access services

- [ ] indexing/abstracting services in this list will also cover material in the "separate" that is co-published simultaneously with Haworth's special thematic journal issue or DocuSerial. Indexing/abstracting usually covers material at the article/chapter level.

- [ ] monographic co-editions are intended for either non-subscribers or libraries which intend to purchase a second copy for their circulating collections.

- [ ] monographic co-editions are reported to all jobbers/wholesalers/approval plans. The source journal is listed as the "series" to assist the prevention of duplicate purchasing in the same manner utilized for books-in-series.

- [ ] to facilitate user/access services all indexing/abstracting services are encouraged to utilize the co-indexing entry note indicated at the bottom of the first page of each article/chapter/contribution.

- [ ] this is intended to assist a library user of any reference tool (whether print, electronic, online, or CD-ROM) to locate the monographic version if the library has purchased this version but not a subscription to the source journal.

- [ ] individual articles/chapters in any Haworth publication are also available through the Haworth Document Delivery Services (HDDS).

DEDICATION

This special volume on women and disability is dedicated to my cousin Jean, who died in 1992 from complications of multiple sclerosis, having lived her life richly and fully; and whose example taught me much.

Mary E. Willmuth

Women with Disabilities: Found Voices

CONTENTS

Introduction   1
    Michelle Fine

The Celebration of the Passage of the Americans
    with Disabilities Act   7
    Patricia Ranzoni

Coming Out in Voices   9
    Laura Hershey

Survival   19
    Lilly Friedman

Double Bind Messages: The Effects of Attitude Towards
    Disability on Therapy   29
    Geri Esten
    Lynn Willmott

The Prize: Disability, Parenthood, and Adoption   43
    Jane Zirinsky-Wyatt

Women Who Are Visually Impaired or Blind as Psychotherapy
    Clients: A Personal and Professional Perspective   55
    Mary Harsh

The Common Agenda Between Old Women, Women
    with Disabilities and All Women   65
    Shevy Healey

Looking Through the Mirror of Disability: Transference
    and Countertransference Issues with Therapists
    Who Are Disabled   79
    Alison G. Freeman

Women and Physical Distinction: A Review of the Literature
and Suggestions for Intervention   91
    Sondra E. Solomon

An Account of the Search of a Woman Who Is Verbally
Impaired for Augmentative Devices to End Her Silence   105
    Lisa Fay

What We Know About Women's Technology Use, Avoidance,
and Abandonment   117
    Marcia J. Scherer

An Open Letter to Health and Mental Health Care
Professionals from a Survivor of Sexual Exploitation   133
    Martha E. Sheldon

Sexually Abused Women with Mental Retardation: Hidden
Victims, Absent Resources   139
    Marilyn M. Stromsness

Further Labeling Within the Category of Disability Due
to Chemical Dependency: Borderline Personality Disorder   153
    Gloria J. Hamilton

Another Strand of Our Diversity: Some Thoughts
from a Feminist Therapist with Severe Chronic Illness   159
    Jessica M. Barshay

Environmental Illness/Multiple Chemical Sensitivities:
Invisible Disabilities   171
    Pamela Reed Gibson

Disability in Female Immigrants with Ritually Inflicted
Genital Mutilation   187
    Hanny Lightfoot-Klein

Found Voices: Women, Disability and Cultural
Transformation   195
    Deborah Lisi

SURVIVING SALEM with a movement disorder
and several witches' tits   211
    Patricia Ranzoni

ABOUT THE EDITORS

Mary E. Willmuth, PhD, is a licensed psychologist who works in rehabilitation where she has daily contact with women with disabilities. She is Clinical Associate Professor at the University of Vermont where she teaches graduate students, medical students, and residents. As a therapist, supervisor, and teacher, she seeks to attend to and educate others about gender issues in rehabilitation.

Lillian P. Holcomb, PhD, is a licensed psychologist in practice at the Ola Hou Clinic in Pearl City, Hawaii, where she specializes in work with people with disabilities, women's issues, and aging. She is particularly interested in how these concerns interact, especially in terms of poverty and crisis intervention. Previously, Dr. Holcomb was Professor at the University of Hawaii (Manoa) Women's Studies Program and Director of the Women's Center at the University of Hawaii/Leeward Campus.

ACKNOWLEDGEMENTS

The editors wish to acknowledge the support of the Medical Center Hospital of Vermont in the preparation and completion of this special volume on women and disability. In particular, the assistance and help with organizational and secretarial tasks given by Barbara Jones was invaluable and very much appreciated throughout what turned out to be a lengthy project.

Introduction

Michelle Fine

As I sit to construct an introduction fitting to this delicious, painful and stirring set of essays, I glance at the newspaper, covering the story of rape of a young woman, age 17 at the time, legally classified as having mental retardation, by a group of four plus young, white males, in their basement. Serial fellatio, insertions of brooms and bats are acknowledged by all. The defense calls her the "suburban Lolita," and brings forth a "history of promiscuity." The prosecution paints her a pitiful "misfit" with the "mind of a child." The psychologist for the young woman tries to interrupt the abusive discourse which justifies male violence, and tries to tame the patronizing, perhaps equally violent discourse, which paints the young woman as, simply, an invalid, or in-valid. But the "best" her side can do is represent her as unable to provide consent, even if consent were "apparent" to the young men. In the words of the young woman, she couldn't say No, they seemed to just expect it. She wanted to be liked so much. And she told her parents she wanted to kill herself a week after the incident.

Michelle Fine, PhD, is Professor of Social Psychology at the Graduate Center/ CUNY. She is author of *Family Dropouts: Notes on the Politics of an Urban High School* (SUNY, 1991), and *Disruptive Voices* (U. Michigan Press, 1992), and co-author (with Adrienne Asch) of *Women with Disabilities* (Temple University Press, 1988).

Address correspondence to: Michelle Fine, PhD, The Graduate School and University Center of the City University of New York, PhD Program in Psychology: Social-Personality Psychology/Box 325, Graduate Center, 33 West 42 Street, New York, NY 10036-8099.

[Haworth co-indexing entry note]: "Introduction." Fine, Michelle. Co-published simultaneously in *Women & Therapy* (The Haworth Press, Inc.) Vol. 14, No. 3/4, 1993, pp. 1-5; and: *Women with Disabilities: Found Voices* (ed: Mary E. Willmuth, and Lillian Holcomb) The Haworth Press, Inc., 1993, pp. 1-5. Multiple copies of this article/chapter may be purchased from The Haworth Document Delivery Center [1-800-3-HAWORTH; 9:00 a.m. - 5:00 p.m. (EST)].

We sit, surrounded by equally violent images that justify male sexual violence because she "wanted it" and those that patronize away this young woman's agency, desires, subjectivity because she has a disability. Interruption seems almost impossible. But then I got to indulge in the essays you are about to read, and interruption leaps from these texts.

The set of articles which follow reveal, in deeply personal, closely technical and sometimes theoretical terms, a thoroughing interruption of popular, disability rights and even feminist discourse on the body, violence, sexuality and disabilities. A talented set of writers, who bring all kinds of differences in disabilities, races, ethnicities, sexualities and politics to this material, collectively force readers to grapple with our own (those of us non-disabled especially), preconceptions, misgivings, difficulties, anxieties, middle age fears, bodily indulgences.

These essays, tough going as they can be, deliver to readers a sense of rich, political possibility. Written almost entirely by women who live with disabilities, within a disability phobic culture, the words carry critique but also a solid desire for coalition building and activism. Deborah Lisi writes about her interviews with a series of women with disabilities:

> These are new voices calling, cajoling and singing to be heard. But it is a struggle to be heard. It is a struggle to hear your own voice when the experience you bring to the world is not one that others share . . . Most of the women I spoke to saw themselves as rebels.

Voices of rebellion, resistance and refusal sparkle across these essays. The refusal to accept medical definitions of "success" is articulated by Lisa Fay, a verbally impaired woman in "search" of augmentative devices to end her silence:

> A revolution in my own thinking took place over 20 years. From childhood, I was taught to speak regardless of the effort it entailed or how I was feeling about treatment. An incident occurring in November 1990 was the straw that broke the camel's back. I called a Boston publisher to encourage him to publish a poetry anthology. When I got him on the phone, he

said, "Speak, speak." The way he said it stuck in my brain. I could not speak automatically when I wanted to speak.

I can no longer go along with what the medical community wants of me, and that is more therapy. Speech therapists think that if I have more therapy then I won't need a device . . . But having more therapy is futile . . . Women are often afraid to say No.

In her remarkable piece, Fay forces readers to acknowledge the sanity of refusal, the insanity of compliance.

In common spirit, if quite different context, Jane Zirinsky-Wyatt writes of her resistance against the adoption agencies who refused to work with her, and her partner, because of the combination of their dual disabilities, and their being an interracial couple.

Even more sobering, Hanny Lightfoot-Klein narrates stories of women who have suffered ritually inflicted genital mutilation as a cultural script subscribed to, and practiced by women and men in some African communities. In these communities resistance is a violation of culture, and an invitation to personal and financial vulnerabilities for self and kin. And yet the gendered pains and costs exacted by these women compel the author to incite, provoke and demand a social revolution by, for and about these women.

The voices of resistance, possibility and activism, resonate proudly across these texts; listen to Laura Hershey:

I have a physical disability which is considered severe, as it restricts my bodily movement so completely. Using resources and supports such as attendant care; an electric breath-operated wheelchair; a voice-activated computer, and other adapted equipment, I live independently, work as a free-lance writer, advocate for my rights and give and receive love and friendship. All of these are acts of rebellion, because I live in a culture mystified by overwhelmingly negative or at least destructive stereotypes of people with disabilities . . . My life itself is an argument against cliche.

As you will see, these texts jolt anti-disability consciousness so that readers must contend with the ways in which disability has been constructed, disguised, rendered disgusting, and, as such, perverted.

But these essays are not simply celebrations, or critique. They advance two other agendas as well. They document, in painful detail, the abuses suffered on the bodies of women with disabilities, including father incest, institutional sexual assault, medical abuse, and cultural mutilation. Further, across essays, we are forced to grapple with the contradictions of being women, of varied colors and classes, with bodies that don't "fit." These are the contradictions of survival in a culture that wishes you dead.

These contradictions constitute the "next" generation of theoretical, practical and political issues for feminists committed to disability studies. These writers deliver, for instance, a set of paradoxes that discomfort. An analysis of the advances of technologies, displays how myths of perfection are built into science. Another admits that she did ask to "die" just following her brutal car accident, but retrospectively, delights in the pleasures of survival, throwing into turmoil all sides of "right to die" arguments. Some of these writers argue that women with disabilities "deny" their vulnerabilities to violence, while others complain that overprotectiveness remains a problem. Some call for a "coming out" of disability and feminist consciousness, while others seek to "move beyond" a fixation on disability and gender toward a more "human outlook." Some argue for a "differences" perspective, others seek to find "similarities." Some insist on analyses which attend to race and ethnicity, and others remain silent–defaulting to whiteness–on the topic.

I take these contradictions to be the core of our intellectual and political work percolating at the nexus of disability studies and feminism. No longer merely documenting the atrocities (an essential phase in the intellectual biography growth of any field); no longer writing celebratory pieces on survival, transcendence and strengths, we are now struggling beyond binary oppositions. The silences have been broken, the violence exposed, the strengths flourishing, and the struggle is on. These essays are an invitation for theoretical, therapeutic and political coalition building; an invitation to those of us disabled, and those not yet disabled, to incite a politic of resistance for women, across and within the many bodies we inhabit.

Enjoy the essays, and as you read them, let us keep imagining how to interrupt the courtroom scene in Newark, New Jersey, where the discourse on gender, sex and disability has regressed by 20 years, and where pains flood the body of a young woman caught at the painful intersection of gender and disability oppression. She needs us to keep interrupting, just as we need her sincerity and strength to remember why the struggle must persist in theory, and in praxis.

The Celebration of the Passage of the Americans with Disabilities Act

Patricia Ranzoni

When the neurological disorder, torsion dystonia, began threatening her speech and motor control in 1983, Pat Ranzoni, an 8th generation Hancock County woman, turned to computer writing as a primary means of expression. In addition to publications on her work as an education consultant and mental health counselor, Ranzoni found poetry helpful in coming to terms with changing views on life and language. She and her husband live with a flocklet of chickens and other creatures of the fields and woods on a homestead in Bucksport, Maine.

Jean Stewart lifts herself from wheelchair to stool and reads for Women's History Month, University of Maine.

in celebration of the passage of the Americans With Disabilities Act

You could tell the ones who know
what you wheel for the academics
turning in surprise to our outbursts and applause
for your work on the ADA: sweet sweat of liberation
christening the threshold of the Center for the Arts
whose director wasn't interested in Access Theater's

Correspondence may be addressed to: Patricia Smith Ranzoni, Star Route Box 173, Bucksport, ME 04416. © Patricia Ranzoni

[Haworth co-indexing entry note]: "The Celebration of the Passage of the Americans with Disabilities Act." Ranzoni, Patricia. Co-published simultaneously in *Women & Therapy* (The Haworth Press, Inc.) Vol. 14, No. 3/4, 1993, pp. 7-8; and: *Women with Disabilities: Found Voices* (ed: Mary E. Willmuth, and Lillian Holcomb) The Haworth Press, Inc., 1993, pp. 7-8. Multiple copies of this article/chapter may be purchased from The Haworth Document Delivery Center [1-800-3-HAWORTH; 9:00 a.m. - 5:00 p.m. (EST)].

dystonic *Storm Reading* last year. They'll probably
break in with deaf theater we decided or something less
shocking to the campus community whose president
told our marchers the year before: "It's hard
raising money for something like that." (Access. To classes.)

Well we've made it to a side space
if not the stage and the same tired tears of joy
that didn't show beneath your raised fist
on the front page of the *New York Times* spring in me
long lost sister you wrote. And when you read
you grabbed me by the guts and I was no longer alone
before the town council down river the only one
to testify to their indifference the only one
to demand entrance to upper rooms. No longer alone linked
to the chain in the rotunda of acting out crips gimps
freaks refusing to keep our place. No longer!

When you signed a poem to me my body "jerk[ing]
like rabbits just hit by cars,"* your eyes
                    your eyes
sent fierce infusions of strength and belief
your whole being in elegant lean found my wounds
and locked
        locked
my hope to yours a goddess lifting me
your searing silence speaking as if you knew
                    as if you knew
how much I needed you to know.
Do you understand ? your movements
implored. Your veins and skin flashing fire.
Do you understand?

---

* From *The Body's Memory,* a novel by Jean Stewart. St. Martins Press, 1989.

Coming Out in Voices

Laura Hershey

SUMMARY. This paper articulates the personal experiences of a woman with a physical disability who enters therapy to explore issues involving lesbian identity, health and illness, disability oppression and pride, and relationships. Written in the first person, the article uses anecdotes, poetry, and journal entries to chart the author's process of self-discovery. As a woman, a lesbian, and a person with a disability, the author frequently finds herself at odds with the culture around her. This creates conflicts between the author's real self, and the self she must present to others. She discusses how she had learned to "silence the voices" which were not useful in challenging stereotypes, making others comfortable, or communicating with assistants. The author describes how therapy offered her the opportunity to unlearn the silence, value all of her voices, listen to herself, resolve her internal dilemmas, and develop a deeper sense of self.

I have *come out* many times in my life, and I'm still doing so. My voice, my writing, is the profoundest and truest way that my various selves become apparent to me and to others, and this is neverend-

Laura Hershey has published articles, performed poetry, and demonstrated for justice throughout the United States. She writes a monthly column for the *Denver Post*, contributes frequently to *Disability Rag*, and has created two audiotapes of her poetry, *The Prostitutes of Nairobi* and *You Get Proud By Practicing*. She was recently awarded an honorary doctorate from Colorado College in recognition of her effective activism.

Correspondence may be addressed to: Laura Hershey, 1466 South Lincoln Street, Denver, CO 80210.

[Haworth co-indexing entry note]: "Coming Out in Voices." Hershey, Laura. Co-published simultaneously in *Women & Therapy* (The Haworth Press, Inc.) Vol. 14, No. 3/4, 1993, pp. 9-17; and: *Women with Disabilities: Found Voices* (ed: Mary E. Willmuth, and Lillian Holcomb) The Haworth Press, Inc., 1993, pp. 9-17. Multiple copies of this article/chapter may be purchased from The Haworth Document Delivery Center [1-800-3-HAWORTH; 9:00 a.m. - 5:00 p.m. (EST)].

ing. I am constantly amazed at the number of situations in which I must make the choice to come out or not, and the tremendous amount of energy involved in making, and then implementing, this choice. Two years ago I made another choice: to seek a therapist who could help support my coming out process*es* (plural).

As a writer and activist, I thought I was already saying everything I needed to say. My outlook and my testimony were clear, public, acutely political, self-defensive. I was and am intensely concerned with educating and enlightening other people to my reality, and this is an enormous challenge.

I have a physical disability which is considered severe, as it restricts my bodily movement so completely. Using resources and supports such as attendant care; an electric, breath-operated wheel-chair; a voice-activated computer; and other adapted equipment, I live independently, work as a free-lance writer, advocate for my rights, and give and receive love and friendship. All of these are acts of rebellion, because I live in a culture mystified by over-whelmingly negative or at least destructive stereotypes of people with disabilities.

I look around me, and see all these distorted reflections of who I am assumed to be. I see children on TV, begging for money in the richest country on earth; and I see muscular men leaving their wheelchairs on the ground as they climb mountains. I see fictional characters whose disabilities are exploited as metaphors. I see media-friendly disabled people who find religion, and with it a passive complacency about the barriers here on Earth. I see journalists, lawyers, and disabled people themselves, arguing for the "right to die," and implying that the natural response to disability is suicide. I do not see anything recognizably close to who I am, or want to be.

And so, faced with such images, I constantly put myself forward, as many disability activists do, as proof that the stereotypes are false. Dedicated to changing other people's attitudes, I seek every day to show and tell my competence, my positive acceptance of disability, my hardiness, my self-respect, and my similarity to the rest of the human race. I reject, as if my life depended on it–which it does–the conventional views of people with disabilities as pathetic, despondent, cursed, and infirm. I do so in my writing, in speeches, in all my actions and interactions. My life itself is an argument against cliché.

(It was this necessary, defensive posture which had previously kept me from seeing how therapy might enhance my life. I had heard horror stories from friends with disabilities. They had sought support, but found instead therapists who held the same stereotypes and misconceptions as the rest of society. I feared I would have to spend precious time and money educating a therapist about the realities of disability. In fact, when I began therapy with Zee, I did find myself "testing" her awareness level. Luckily for me, she usually passed.)

My carefully constructed persona, my model of calm, competence, and confidence, has worked reasonably well throughout my life, making possible a degree of acceptance and success during college and the first few years of my professional career. But the energy expenditure such efforts require has taken a toll on me, both physically and emotionally. Health problems finally forced me to a decision about what was really important in my life. I left a high-profile, high-stress, full-time job as a disability-rights advocate in city government. I started working at home as a free-lance writer. At the same time, I was exploring deeper commitment within my first-ever serious love relationship. With these and other changes buffeting me and my usual unshakable equilibrium, I decided to begin therapy.

At the time, I wasn't sure exactly what I needed. I *was* sure I wanted a woman therapist, not because I particularly distrust men, but because I generally feel a deeper connection with women. I also knew that my new relationship, my sexual awakening, and confrontations with homophobia would be among my issues–and so I sought a referral from my local gay/lesbian community center for a lesbian therapist.

Zee was honest with me from the start about her lack of experience with disability. She didn't claim any "expertise" about disability; nor did she bring preconceived notions about it. She told me her approach would be to listen, and to follow my cues about what I needed from her.

I was wary, not only because she was non-disabled, but also because of the situation. Like many people with disabilities, especially women with disabilities, I have endured my share of abuse from the medical field. Visiting Zee's office, sitting in a waiting room, seeing diplomas on the wall, telling all about myself and knowing nothing of her–in other words, all the aspects which smacked of medical professionalism–did make me uneasy. Only time, work, and several leaps of faith on my part, allowed my qualms to give way to her manifest respect and persistent sensitivity.

In Zee's office, I found an opening of some of the voices I had always kept silent. All the selves I had ever fully known were the selves I introduce to other people. These voices give evidence that I am not to be categorized by my disability, and not to be pitied. These voices are political; they are fine-tuned and articulate. They are also the skillful, diplomatic voices of one who must rely on others to meet many of her basic needs for personal care and daily functioning.

But now I needed to let my other voices come out. I needed to come out.

By *coming out*, I mean much more than simply acknowledging that I am a lesbian, although that is part of it. To speak the truth about one's own sexuality, in a culture steeped in an impersonal, conformist sexuality, is risky for anyone. For me as a woman with a disability, such truth carries double shock value. Most people are assumed to be heterosexual unless they announce otherwise. People with disabilities are assumed to be asexual. Throughout my childhood and adulthood, I received very few messages, public or private, suggesting that I would ever have an intimate sexual relationship. When I did, and when that relationship was with another woman, my process of coming out challenged two very deep-seated prejudices.

Other comings out have marked my path as well. My physical disability is so obvious an attribute, so inconcealable, that "coming out" about it would seem, to some, redundant. But how I present myself, in relation to my disability, is very much a matter of choice. I could choose, as I did throughout high school and college, to present a view to others which minimizes the impact of disability on my life, which downplays my own needs arising from my disability, which tacitly disclaims any affinity with a community of people with disabilities, and which essentially denies my reality as being different from the non-disabled people around me. This approach has several attractions. It emphasizes sameness, rather than difference, among people, thus softening potential frictions. It avoids, or at least delays, the difficult political responsibilities made necessary by those differences and frictions. And it tries to make other people more comfortable, by keeping disability as a private problem, rather than a shared, social predicament.

This approach has several drawbacks too, however, just as being a closeted lesbian has drawbacks which usually outweigh considerations of safety and comfort. There's a certain controlled insanity which goes along with not being honest about who you are and what you need in order to survive and be happy in life. I still find myself pretending when I have to, or when I think I have to.

Here is a good example. Let's say someone wants to schedule a meeting with me at 7 a.m. Rather than explain that I would have to get up at 4 a.m., which would tire me out for the rest of the day, and that I can't get an attendant to work that early anyway, I might instead tell them I have a conflicting appointment. Or I might call all my back-up attendants until I can schedule someone, and go ahead and get up that early, disregarding how it might affect my health. Telling the truth might feel like too much exposure, too clear a picture of my real self, which includes limitations. It might reveal too clearly my dissimilarity from the person with whom I am speaking, making communion between us impossible. This is not so different from stashing away the gay magazines when certain people visit my house. It just avoids a whole lot of explanation and tension.

But when those contradictions become too troublesome, I find some way to come out. I march for Gay Pride. I demand access. I introduce Robin as my partner. I take a day off when I need to. And I open my voices, in poetry or explanation or chant, or perhaps only in therapy.

When I began therapy, one of my fears was that Zee would make assumptions about the impact of disability on my life, over-estimating its importance in shaping my issues. I was assuming that disability would be a minor factor, an infrequent topic in our sessions. As it turned out, I was the one who kept bringing up disability-related problems and issues. By listening so non-judgmentally, Zee gave me a space in which to value that aspect of my experience, and to validate my own reactions to it. I found new voices–of anger, of joy, of sadness, of reflection, of fear, of pain, of creative growth, of need.

These voices may or may not echo the positive projected images I've often led others to expect from me. They may or may not be politically useful. But more and more, they are more truly me. And so my coming out is taking on deeper tones of truthfulness, and illuminating new facets of myself.

Living with a disability is a complex endeavor requiring almost constant communication. Attendants, friends, strangers, co-workers, and family members must all be dealt with in the context of the disability. For me, this has resulted both in a fine-tuning of some of my voices, as I acquired effective communication skills, and in a silencing of other voices. I grew apart from those voices which would not be useful in political advocacy, or in supervising my attendants, or in making other people comfortable with my disability.

When I first began therapy with Zee, I communicated with her in much the same way I communicate with others. I scrupulously presented myself as essentially "normal"; I played down my differences; I carefully gauged her responses to me; and I sought frequent feedback from her to prompt or shape my own discourse. I also assumed she would have the usual misconceptions and stereotypes about people with disabilities, and I stayed on guard for this, ready to correct her if necessary.

Gradually, however, as trust developed, my own need for expression became more important than my concern for Zee's reactions. In other words, I focused my attention more on what I was saying than on what she might be hearing or thinking. This felt really extraordinary to me! For so long, my own words had been subtly but profoundly influenced by the reactions of others, by the needs of others, or simply by the presence of others. Now I was seeing what it felt like to express something from deep inside myself, which had absolutely nothing to do with the other. I believe this experience deeply affected my consciousness about myself. About a year after starting therapy, I wrote a poem called "You Get Proud By Practicing," which has become one of my own favorites. In it I wrote, "There are many many ways to get proud." In listing some of the ways, I included the following statement which I think describes what I got from Zee:

> You can find someone
> who will listen to you
> without judging you or doubting you or being
> afraid of you
> and let you hear yourself perhaps
> for the first time.

This hasn't happened all the time in my therapy. Old habits die hard. Sometimes I still unintentionally muffle key voices. I wonder: Is this making sense to her? How does she see/hear me? Can she possibly understand this? Is this weird? I solicit her feedback, needing external confirmation that I'm on the right track.

At other times, though, we create together a space in which my truest voices come out almost unimpeded. At such times, talking feels both intense and oddly effortless at the same time. At such times, I will occasionally feel so absorbed in revealing myself to myself, that I am startled when Zee makes a comment of her own. On later examination, her remark usually offers a helpful insight; but at the time, it feels like an interruption. This particular experience has become a clue for me that a session is going well, that it will yield a nourishing dose of self-knowledge.

In the process, I am learning to hear and honor my various voices, and the differences among them. I begin to understand when and how they developed, how they strengthen and/or limit me, and what they might have to say to me. For example, the following journal entry describes an incident that occurred when I went to a hospital for a routine test. I saw a terrified little girl desperately resisting the tyranny of medical procedures:

> I felt like telling them to leave her alone, let her go home. I know I saw in her fear my own childhood traumas, the many times I faced those hard tables and unforgiving machines. I remember that desperate attempted rebellion against efficient people who had a job to do, who would not be thwarted by a child's uncontrolled crying. I want to write a poem about it. At the time, I had to suppress my uneasiness, had to stay calm and

present for my own appointment so I could ask the right questions, and give instructions to the technicians about how best to move me, how to adapt their usual procedures to my own unusual requirements.

Those two different voices–the child's wailing and the adult's patient explanation–had for so long been kept apart in me. Zee and I explored the incident, and the memories it evoked, in therapy. I wrote a long poem, "Little Girl You Are My Voice," in which I addressed both the child I saw in the waiting room *and* the child I once was:

> i once knew
> like you
> how to let the fear rooted in my heart branch
> from my mouth break open leaves earthdeep wallshaking
> howls
> i lost that pain somewhere
> in myself

And in the poem, I called for the rejoining of the two voices:

> let it now emerge
>
> little girl you are my voice
> let me be for you language
>
> these walls of white and number
> our words stir
> yes
> our words our questions our truth
>
> little girl
> let us speak

Some of my selves want to speak of fear, anger, self-doubt, sadness, and other emotions previously censored for the sake of survival. Therapy for me has meant hearing and understanding those other voices. To my surprise, opening these voices has often yielded strength, even as they revealed vulnerability. And, contrary to what I half expected, I am not becoming apolitical by focusing on my more personal, emotional self. Rather, my politics are deepening. I become more passionate and committed as I speak from a medley of true voices. For example, my anger over incidents of discrimination and exclusion now resonates from within. My emotional self is no longer an awkward stranger, but a source of power.

I am allowing all my voices to come out, and I am thereby continuing to come out.

Survival

Lilly Friedman

SUMMARY. This article describes the trauma and subsequent struggle of surviving a serious car accident. It deals with the physical efforts to keep me alive as well as the emotional impact and suffering.

I was an "active sixty-three" when my life changed drastically. The car I drove en route to a vacation unexplainedly swerved, landed in a ditch and rolled over. I became QUADRIPLEGIC in one instant–paralyzed from the neck down, permanently confined to a wheelchair.

I spent several unforgettable months in a Florida hospital, hooked up to life supports, hovering between life and death. I was then flown to New York for rehabilitation. A devoted medical team and supportive family taught me to become somewhat independent with the help of high-tech equipment, preparing me to face the world as a "QUAD."

Six years have passed and I still mourn my "body beautiful," but I have accepted my limitations and found new challenges in life.

Life as I used to know it drastically changed for me five years ago when I unexplainedly lost control of the car I drove and rolled over several times before coming to a halt. I survived, but sustained serious injuries, a broken neck and severed spinal cord, leaving me paralyzed from the neck down. In one brief moment I became QUADRIPLEGIC, permanently, totally disabled.

Lilly Friedman, at sixty-three, survived a serious car accident which left her totally paralyzed. This is her story.

Correspondence may be addressed to: Lilly Friedman, RR 1, Box 107, Wilmington, VT 05363.

[Haworth co-indexing entry note]: "Survival." Friedman, Lilly. Co-published simultaneously in *Women & Therapy* (The Haworth Press, Inc.) Vol. 14, No. 3/4, 1993, pp. 19-27; and: *Women with Disabilities: Found Voices* (ed: Mary E. Willmuth, and Lillian Holcomb) The Haworth Press, Inc., 1993, pp. 19-27. Multiple copies of this article/chapter may be purchased from The Haworth Document Delivery Center [1-800-3-HAWORTH; 9:00 a.m. - 5:00 p.m. (EST)].

At the time of the accident I was sixty-three. In comparison to some of my contemporaries I looked at least ten years younger. I dressed smartly, liked the sophisticated look. Physically I was in good shape. Being tall (5'8") and slim I never had to fight "the battle of the bulge." My favorite sports were sailing, skiing and tennis. I volunteered in women's organizations most of my adult life. I felt great satisfaction in tackling any job as long as the work was varied. I considered myself "Jack of all trades, master of none." My husband had just retired from his management consulting practice in which I was active, my two daughters were married and had started their own families, and my mother who lived with us for seventeen years had passed away. I felt my role of caretaker would diminish, and I could become more carefree. We had moved from New Jersey to Vermont, planning to spend summers near our children and grandchildren and winters in Florida. These were going to be the "golden" years, the best of my life. And then it all happened . . . .

It was December third, 1986, early afternoon. My husband and I were ready for our annual trip South, leaving behind snow and ice in Vermont, heading for sunny Florida. The house shut tight for the duration, the Audi and Mercedes packed to capacity, we left the WATER LILLY HAUS with our customary quote: "We're off!"

We spent the night in New Jersey and on December fourth continued to Washington for an overnight trip on the autotrain.

Next morning, December fifth, we got into Orlando, Florida. After having retrieved our cars, we drove a short distance to have lunch with a longtime friend, reminiscing and recalling old times. Refreshed and anxious to get to our destination, we soon were on our way to Singer Island, ready to start "winter life" in Florida. Within two hours we'd be there, open the hurricane shutters and let in light and the sound of the surf. It was a hot, humid day, and I couldn't wait to take off the heavy clothes, get into a bathing suit, and take that first dip in the ocean.

Early afternoon on the Florida Turnpike, I drove the Audi on cruise control, seat belt fastened, my husband right behind me in the Mercedes. All of a sudden–a tremendous jolt! CRASH . . . BANG. . . I wasn't sure what had happened. I was turning and tumbling, rising, falling–then came to a stop. I was conscious and aware of still being in the car, but felt upside down . . . I heard a voice: "Don't move,

we'll get you out–you're trapped in the car. You had an accident!"
It was my husband trying to comfort me. I felt a stabbing pain in my
neck, a roaring noise in my ears–panic. I suddenly recalled a similar
sensation years ago when swimming in the ocean, not far from the
shore. I got caught in an undertow, going down, down . . . What was
happening now? . . . Dimly I heard other voices. A trucker had
stopped and attempted to pull me out but couldn't reach me. An
emergency wrecker arrived and literally cut me out of the car with
saws. The Audi was a total wreck. The roof was smashed in and
broken glass everywhere. Yet I did not have one scratch–ONLY A
BROKEN NECK! I remember repeating "Help me, help me, I'm in
such pain." I never lost consciousness, but things were blurry
around me. After what seemed an eternity, an ambulance with si-
rens at full blast rushed me to the nearest hospital about 15 miles
from the scene of the accident.

Almost immediately after arriving at Lawnwood Hospital, doctors and nurses began hovering over me discussing my case. As a
result of the accident my spinal cord had been severed at the high
level of C-5/6 causing very serious injuries. The diagnosis was:
QUADRIPLEGIA. It meant permanent paralysis from the neck
down. I would never walk again or ever regain the use of my hands.
In one brief moment, when my car ran off the road and into a ditch,
flipping over 2-1/2 times, I had become "QUAD."

The neurosurgeon and his team debated whether to surgically
fuse my spine or just align it. They decided not to operate but put
me into a bed that automatically rotated 180 degrees every 15
minutes, making me face either the floor or the ceiling. It felt like
being strapped onto a roller coaster, constantly moving back and
forth, up and down. To keep the spine straight, they fitted me with a
"halo," a padded harness over the head, shoulders and chest, and to
hold that contraption in place two holes were drilled into my skull
and large screws inserted. I felt crucified. I was also hooked up to a
respirator supplying me with oxygen because my lungs had partially
collapsed.

One of my biggest frustrations was that I couldn't speak. A
tracheotomy had been performed in order for me to breathe, but the
tube the doctors inserted into my throat temporarily paralyzed my
vocal cords and prevented me from uttering a sound. The only way

I could communicate was by blinking my left eye for "yes" and my right eye for "no." Terrific! They put a board in front of me with five letters on a line, starting with A to E on the first line, and so on throughout the alphabet. They pointed to each letter and by blinking an eye I indicated the letters that spelled what I had to say. One sentence took about 5 minutes, but I was able to convey my basic needs and thoughts.

Those first days in the hospital seemed like a bad dream. Heavy doses of morphine helped dull any pain in my head but prevented me from distinguishing reality from fantasy. I had a recurring nightmare: A small group of people dressed in costumes was standing around me in a circle, staring at me, touching me. I particularly remember one man who had a sign painted on his forehead; it resembled the symbol of lightning, very frightening. The men talked to each other in a language I couldn't understand. From the hospital room they repeatedly led me through a dark tunnel to their native village. In full view of the entire tribe they put a tent over my head and filled it with gas; they were going to kill me. I was ready for death at that time. I didn't want to live any longer. I had suffered enough, I was prepared. Yet, I didn't die; I found myself back in my room again. Another time they informed me that one of their men urgently needed a heart transplant and I seemed the perfect available donor. Even though I was prepared to die, my subconscious told me this was no way to go. I pointed out to them that I had a prolapse of the mitral valve and therefore my heart would be of no use to anyone. They had a short discussion among themselves and agreed to scrap that plan. But a few days later they took me through the tunnel again. At the other end I saw a sudden bright light, heard drums beating. The entire tribe was dancing in a circle. Men, women and children were drinking and chanting while building a wooden stake. It dawned upon me that I was to be the victim! Just before lighting the fire a sheriff appeared and I implored him to save my life. He assured me he had some influence with the chief and would do everything he could to help me, but first he had to take a "lunch break." I pleaded with him not to leave me–I was terrified, but he disappeared and never returned. Soon afterwards "my group of Indians" came close to me and said, "You told us several times you don't want to live anymore; we are really here to carry out your wish. Nobody else will help you to die, you should be grateful to us." I guess my instinct for survival took over. I begged them not to burn me at the stake, I wanted to give it another try. I must have convinced them because I found myself back in my room.

After that incident the nightmares stopped. They had seemed so real that I will never forget them. Much later on I found a possible rationale: I was under heavy sedation at that time and the morphine possibly caused hallucinations. The frightening trips through the tunnel were probably my repeated experiences in the tube of a CT scanner. This entire incident could have passed through my mind within a few hours or days, I don't know, but it is as real to me today as it was then.

Those first two weeks were intolerable. I was lying there, hooked up to life-sustaining equipment, paralyzed from the neck down and unable to communicate except by rolling or blinking an eye. In sign language I begged the doctor to turn off the respirator and let me go; I had suffered enough, I just wanted to die in peace. I remember that he looked down on me in silence and then said, "I hear you and understand what you are asking of me. Considering your serious condition and frankly poor prognosis, I would go along with your decision, however, only under one condition: your husband has to come to me and say, "Do it" and this has to be in writing. I cannot risk it any other way."

Even though I was conscious at all times, I didn't really know what was going on around me. I was totally unaware that my husband had just undergone an emergency open heart by-pass operation and was in an intensive-care unit in another hospital nearby. I vaguely remember my two daughters and their husbands visiting me daily and wondered why they didn't go home. When I questioned them about why their father didn't come to see me, they told me he had a cold and for "my sake" wasn't coming to the hospital. Apparently I was so absorbed with "me only" that I didn't doubt that explanation.

I know that I tried repeatedly to convey to my children that I had nothing to live for, to please let me go and stop all this unbearable suffering. But of course they would not hear of my giving up. "We love you, Mom, Dad needs you, your grandchildren want you. You can't give up, give it a chance, please! You are a survivor, keep fighting, you'll be O.K." . . . I promised and held on.

After hovering between life and death for about a month, I was transferred to Jupiter Hospital which was closer to home and a much larger and better-equipped facility. I had my own room and could receive visitors at any time. The "steel halo and armor" were still screwed to my head and neck; I could not turn in any direction, but I had regained my speech. Now I could at least communicate and be in touch with the world around me. The staff, nurses, and doctors were trying their best to cheer me up, telling me how much I was improving and that I had come a long way. It didn't seem so to me. I couldn't move except roll my eyes; I felt like a prisoner in my own body. I was very depressed. The only thing that kept me going was my husband, who had recovered from his surgery and came to me daily. He looked haggard and weak from all that had happened, but his optimism and perseverance were still visible. He said the doctors were pleased with my progress. I was now "medically stable" and ready for the next step–rehabilitation. A flurry of activity started in looking for the best "rehab. center" to go to. Our first choice, Jackson Memorial Hospital in Miami, where they do a lot of research about spinal cord injury, turned us down because there was a strike and therefore they were not accepting new patients. Craig in Colorado and other well-known facilities were considered, but they were too far away from home and family. So the Rusk Institute for Rehabilitation in New York City was decided upon.

I was rather surprised when one afternoon the nurses gathered around my bedside carrying a candle-lit cake. It was to be a farewell party for me, their most unusual patient. The head nurse announced that I would leave for New York the next morning. I was a bit apprehensive about leaving the sheltered environment and excellent care I got at Jupiter hospital, yet excited about moving on to the next stage. Later that evening, my husband explained that I would be brought to the nearest airport by ambulance and then be flown in a small, privately chartered airplane to New York. Aside from him, a doctor and a nurse would be in attendance. I had mixed feelings about this flight. An entire plane with me as its only passenger? How much would that cost? All that fuss and I couldn't even enjoy it? Actually I was hardly aware of my surroundings except for much commotion and many transfers on stretchers. They had sedated me before leaving so I would be more "comfortable."

After a long trip we arrived at Rusk Institute for Rehabilitation on 34th Street in Manhattan. Part of the huge New York University hospital complex, it was to be my home for the next five months. Gone was the intimacy of the small hospital. I shared a tiny room with three women whose faces I rarely saw because of my rigid position in bed. Their moaning and groaning was constant. The nurses were over-worked and the aides, who did most of the chores, were grouchy and unwilling to meet my frequent demands. I needed assistance with everything, from feeding and washing to blowing my nose and scratching my head. I did not feel any discrimination as a woman but became painfully aware that I had permanently lost my role as a "care-giver" and my strong instinct to "nurture." In the beginning I had to be turned from side to side every few hours and because of my "dead weight" I was often taken care of by male nurses. At first I resented the "manhandling"–they were young guys in their early twenties just out of school, but they were caring and competent, and I soon looked forward to seeing Jim or Tony at my side to take care of me in the morning. For the first few weeks I had private nurses around the clock which was an expensive luxury but made life a little easier. My husband had rented an efficiency apartment nearby and visited me daily.

My medical condition improved slowly and after a month's stay I was taken off the respirator, the trachea was closed, and my harness, the steel "halo" on my head, was removed. At that point I was thankful for little things. I was now able to move my head and see a bit more of what was going on around me. I was given my first shower in months, a great event! Also, my nurse had rolled me in a wheelchair to the "garden," a small speck of green on the ground floor of the hospital. I took the first breath of fresh (?) air in a long time, free of the antiseptic smell of a hospital room. I discovered that there was a greenhouse on the grounds with exotic tropical plants including beautiful orchids. In one corner I discovered my favorite flowers, fuchsia cyclamen. I couldn't bend down to take in the delicate fragrance, but just looking at them brought back childhood memories of picking them each fall in the woods near my home where they grew in abundance.

During weekdays I had a very busy schedule. From 9 a.m. to 3 p.m. there was physical and occupational therapy where I received intense exercise to my arms and legs. It was hard work, but it paid off; I slowly gained improved function in my upper extremities. I learned "activities for daily living"–how to eat with adaptive arm supports, how to brush my teeth, how to type.

Counseling was provided too. We had group sessions twice a week where we could air our feelings of frustration, anger and hope, and listen to a psychologist's lecture on how to deal with our problems. I always looked forward to those sessions; they were positive and made me realize that I was not alone in my struggle to live with a serious disability. The majority of patients on my floor were young males, injured in motorcycle, car, or diving accidents. I noticed how differently they reacted to being disabled compared to their female counter-parts. They adapted to their condition more easily than women, especially older ones like me. I found they stressed their physical needs and vocalized their concerns over practical matters, while the women readily expressed their feelings and were more emotional. I rarely saw a man cry, whereas the women in our group often broke down and gave way to their frustrations. I felt like their mother and "elder statesman" who had experienced and seen it all. I also thought that women were more conscious of their appearance; they dressed carefully and made attempts to look attractive. How to deal with "sex" after spinal cord injury with a paralyzed body was occasionally touched upon but not freely discussed; I was not ready to talk or even think about the possibility of having sex. I was concerned, however, about the relationship to my husband of thirty-seven years. I had already begun to miss the physical contact. How would my changed body affect us?

I made new friends among my fellow patients. Joey from Kentucky became my pal; he was recovering from a stroke and usually was in an upbeat mood. He told dirty jokes and talked about his horses back home. Then there was Seymour, a native New Yorker. He was the intellectual in our group. He read the New York Times from front to back and kept us informed about "world events." This was especially important to me because I couldn't read yet, and the only stimulus I had at night was watching the sitcoms on TV my roommates insisted on listening to. Seymour called me the "classy lady"–I liked that. I admired Jane for her positive outlook on life. Though paralyzed after a bad fall from a horse at the age of twenty-five and undergoing eight operations to keep her alive, she never gave up hope and had a cheerful smile for anyone who needed encouragement.

The months at Rusk Rehab. actually passed quickly, and one day in July my doctor and medical team informed me that it was time to go home. I had reached a point where they could no longer do anything for me. They had taught me everything to make me as independent as possible. I was outfitted with a power and a manual wheelchair. I was sold high-tech equipment to be installed over my bed so I could handle some basics on my own by blowing into a mouthpiece. It enabled me to make telephone calls, turn on the TV and radio, change positions on my bed. We also bought a converted van to get around in. Gone were the days of driving my Mercedes convertible, hair blowing in the wind! Gone were the days (and nights) of much more.

My feelings about leaving Rusk were understandably ambiguous; in one way I was happy to leave the hospital atmosphere, to start a new phase, but on the other hand I was apprehensive about returning home. It was scary to leave the sheltered environment, the daily routine. How would I fit into my own surroundings, my family and friends of able-bodied people? I was afraid of how I would adjust to living as a "QUAD," how I would cope! Yet I had survived, and I realized that I had to face reality some day.

And so we went home to Vermont . . . .

Double Bind Messages:
The Effects of Attitude
Towards Disability on Therapy

Geri Esten
Lynn Willmott

SUMMARY. This paper illustrates and discusses ways that conflicting communications regarding disability create a double bind for the therapist, the client, or both. The client with a disability finds it difficult to see herself as whole in a society that divides the sick and the healthy into two distinct groups. Due to preconceived attitudes and assumptions, therapists frequently either focus entirely on the disability–reducing the client to a collection of symptoms–or minimize the disability–conveying to the client that she is not acceptable having a disability. Due to their own inability to incorporate their healthy, functioning self with their disability, clients themselves give contradictory messages to how much attention they want paid to

---

Geri Esten is 44 and has had multiple sclerosis for 27 years. She is quadriplegic, blind and has difficulty speaking. She has been a therapist for 22 years, and currently works part-time for the Southern California Chapter of the National Multiple Sclerosis Society leading support groups, as well as training and supervising groups for peer-counselors and professionals. Lynn Willmott is 37 and has had multiple sclerosis for 8 years. Her course with the disease is erratic and unpredictable. She left her former career as a professional chef to pursue a new one in counseling. She has a B.S. in Rehabilitation Counseling and has started graduate work in Social Welfare at the University of California at Los Angeles.

Correspondence may be addressed to: Lynn Willmott, 608 North Beachwood Drive, Los Angeles, CA 90004.

[Haworth co-indexing entry note]: "Double Bind Messages: The Effects of Attitude Towards Disability on Therapy." Esten, Geri, and Lynn Willmott. Co-published simultaneously in *Women & Therapy* (The Haworth Press, Inc.) Vol. 14, No. 3/4, 1993, pp. 29-41; and: *Women with Disabilities: Found Voices* (ed: Mary E. Willmuth, and Lillian Holcomb) The Haworth Press, Inc., 1993, pp. 29-41. Multiple copies of this article/chapter may be purchased from The Haworth Document Delivery Center [1-800-3-HAWORTH; 9:00 a.m. - 5:00 p.m. (EST)].

29

their disability. Thus, both therapist and client create a bind of con-
tradiction which results in uncertainty regarding what is best for the
client to achieve successful integration in therapy; any message left
unclarified will impede–or perhaps destroy–the therapeutic process.
Through citations of personal experiences coupled with references to
existing literature, the authors suggest guidelines for the therapist
working with her client who is disabled.

Disability inevitably creates a double bind in a society which
believes, as John Cheever (1991) has observed, that there is no
greater difference than between the sick and the healthy. Women
who are disabled are very aware that they exist in a world composed
of people who are able-bodied and those who are not. They also
know that their lives consist of more than their disability. However,
contradictory messages make it difficult for the client to see herself
as both fully functioning and disabled–attributes which are usually
treated as separate and mutually exclusive. In therapy both client
and therapist can deliver this problematic communication. When
working with a client with disabilities, a therapist frequently communicates, "I accept you the way you are," yet, at the same time
conveys, "Your disability must be changed because it makes you
unacceptable." On her part, the client says, "Treat me like I'm not
disabled!" but "Don't forget my disability!"

As therapists who are disabled and have been at various times
clients in therapy, we have encountered the following examples of
double bind messages:

1. dispensing the cure;
2. identifying with the client who is disabled;
3. dismissing the disability by suggesting it has psychological
   origins;
4. communicating that a person who is disabled must have lower
   life expectations;
5. meaningless encouragement;
6. problem solving for the client;
7. participating in the denial of the client; and
8. seeing no difference between the person who is disabled and
   one who is not.

Those attitudes and values which a counselor holds may influence success or failure of client outcome (Huitt & Elston, 1991). The following personal experiences, coupled with references from the existing literature, offer explanations of why both subtle and blatant conflicting messages regarding disability can create a double bind.

DISPENSING THE CURE

Therapists frequently fail to see that a person with a disability or chronic illness is not continually thinking about getting better. What often seems to matter most to the therapist is making the client physically well; they forget that the client may have come to therapy to learn how best to live with their disabilities. It is also quite possible that the client has come to therapy to deal with issues which do not stem from the disability at all (Hadley & Brodwin, 1988).

With all good intentions the therapist tells the client of diets, snake venom treatments, special exercise programs, and vitamin regimes that will rid them of the problem. These suggestions communicate that the therapist is the authority and the client is not sufficiently intelligent to comprehend the medical world. Dispensing the cure also carries the unstated message that a person is not all right as long as she is disabled, and if she took better care of herself it would solve the problem. This message instills a sense of guilt and shame in the person with disability and illness (Register, 1987). One of the authors tells of the following experience:

> Once when I was in therapy with a woman I respected very much, she read me an article with great enthusiasm about a diet which purportedly cured multiple sclerosis. She looked up when she finished reading and I was crying. 'How could you?' I said. She had become like everyone else. It was as if she had stopped seeing me and only saw my MS.

This kind of conflicting message from the therapist leaves the client unsure of her true issues, and possibly even unsure of her own identity. She has gone to therapy with the assumption that the therapist will accept her as she is, only to find that acceptance is contingent upon following the therapist's agenda for wellness.

IDENTIFYING

Many therapists feel as though they need to establish a special connection with their client because of their physical disabilities. In our experience, this seems to be more prevalent when a female therapist is working with a female client who is disabled. Their own vulnerability to similar disabilities (Belgrave, 1984; Hartsof, Wildfogal & Cassman, 1979) and the possible loss of "body integrity" (Asch & Rousso, 1985), especially when working with a client similar to them in age and gender, arouses fears which are unsettling. They may try to ease this discomfort by expressing an understanding of disability through their own personal experience. This usually backfires, and can be fatal to the bond between therapist and client. Lynn recalls:

> I had an experience that made me furious with a therapist that I happened to like very much. She was pregnant at the time I was seeing her in a group. She tried so hard to be empathetic by telling me that she was now able to understand what I was going through with my MS because of her discomfort with her pregnancy. She failed to see that her pregnancy was nothing like having a chronic illness that is progressive and without a cure. In several months her discomfort would result in bringing a child into the world, and she would feel just fine again. Not only was I not ever going to feel well again, but my chances of ever having children and being able to raise them like everyone else my age were most likely impossible. The hurt and anger I felt when she said this to me was tremendous— my feelings of being different from my peers, my loss and my pain were still not understood and I was more frustrated than before I started the therapy.

A therapist told Geri she understood what a struggle life could be because she knew how difficult things would be if she went without her glasses for a day. She did not realize that having glasses implied that her vision was correctable; generally a chronic disability is not. Fine and Asch (1988) noted that a person who is not handicapped often " . . . equates having a disability with a bad and eternal flu, toothache, or broken leg . . . It is erroneous for anyone to conclude that their difficulties mirror those of a person who has a long-term disability who has learned to use alternative methods to accomplish the tasks of daily living and working."

Identification is not necessary. Therapist and client do not have to be cut from the same cloth for successful therapy to occur. As is evident from the examples above, the effort of the therapist to identify with the client who is disabled may have the effect of making the client feel less understood and betrayed; if the shared perception of a presumed similarity turns out to be false, the client will doubt what is truly shared between them (Lerman, 1989).

It can also be devastating if the therapist says directly, "I don't know what to say." This slams the door in the client's face by saying that no connection is possible–"You're too different than me, I'll never understand what you're experiencing."

Both of these responses reveal that the therapist is paying attention only to the disability and is very uncomfortable because of it, leaving the client feeling different, bizarre and abnormal. Such special attempts to empathize only serve to further alienate and distance the client from the therapist; rather than bringing the two closer, they emphasize how different they are.

PSYCHOLOGICAL ORIGINS

There is a new philosophy or fad that says that physical problems can result from negative thinking, poor attitude, and deep seated anger. This represents the height of arrogance on the part of the therapist and shows no respect for the client, again by implying that the therapist knows more than the client. It denies the reality of the disability by implying a simple cause-and-effect relationship, and emphasizes failure on the client's part for not being able to heal herself (Register, 1987). Both authors had the experience of being asked what it was they did not want to see when their vision was failing–a common symptom of multiple sclerosis. Geri was told that her disease kept getting worse because her attitude wasn't positive enough, and Lynn is continually told that she must have a great attitude because she is doing so well. In either case, this implies the client is responsible for her disability.

We believe that this says a great deal about the helplessness, denial and discomfort on the part of the therapist. A client with a disability cannot be helped by someone who thinks this way. Being blamed for the disability does not create an atmosphere of feeling free to talk about anything, least of all the feelings about being disabled. There can be no trust when a "blame the victim" approach is taken. Therapists usually know better than to thrust their values of religion or politics on a client; their values about disability and chronic illness should be avoided in the same way.

IMPLYING LOWER EXPECTATIONS

The belief that a person who is disabled must have lower expectations is often communicated by well-intentioned professionals. "Physical incapacities are perceived as leading inevitably to incapacities in other spheres of life" (Fine & Asch, 1988, pg. 13). Such abating statements can be expressly stated as a neurologist did when telling Geri she should begin checking out nursing homes because living independently was not possible, or when a physical therapist in the hospital asked her if she was always in bed at home. When Geri told her that she worked, the therapist asked, "What kind of volunteer work do you do?" Lynn consulted with a social worker for information on possible areas of counseling she could pursue in her new career. The therapist implied that Lynn should go for the easiest possible course of study–if any–not even questioning her about personal preferences and goals. Neither took the advice given; seventeen years later Geri is living in her own home and continues to work as a therapist, and Lynn is currently working on her Masters degree in Social Welfare at a prestigious university. There is an assumption that having a disability is synonymous with needing help and social support, and that less or nothing is expected of them. It is more than possible that the person who has a disability will actually provide these nurturing qualities for others (Fine & Asch, 1988); in fact, they might even become therapists themselves.

The above examples are blatant. More subtle are repeated comments of admiration, particularly of someone who has incurred severe disabilities. Often more positive evaluations of the disabled are given than would be to a non-disabled person in an identical situation (Elliot, MacNair, Herrick, Yoder & Byrne, 1991). Such platitudes often carry the message, "I wouldn't expect that of someone who is disabled." A therapist may sincerely want to give praise for a job well done, or may want to guide her client into making realistic decisions while keeping her disabilities in mind. The client will feel the bind that is created when a therapist imposes limits on the person with disability due to their own stereotypical prejudices and ignorance of their client's true abilities or disabilities. These "less-than-positive attitudes"–as well as comments of excessive admiration and praise elicited by the therapist–hinder the effects of the therapeutic process (Huitt & Elston, 1991), and accentuate the distance between those with disabilities and those without. "Human beings afflicted with illness are no better and no worse, no more heroic and no more cowardly, no stronger and no weaker in spirit than those who live healthy unencumbered lives" (Register, 1987, pg. 30).

MEANINGLESS ENCOURAGEMENT

Sometimes it seems that a therapist wants to help so much that she does not realize that the encouragement given is meaningless, and that it implies that she has absolutely no understanding of what her client is actually feeling. It is condescending and less than truthful to reassure a client that "everything will be okay."

During a counseling group when Lynn expressed her fears about not being able to have children because of difficulties with walking and fatigue, the co-leader of the group–who also had MS–gleefully chimed in and said, "Oh, when I was your age I was having kids and playing tennis." At the time of this group, Lynn was more disabled than the counselor had been at Lynn's age, and Lynn did not care about playing tennis, only about childbearing. The group leader's encouragement of a bright future was not applicable and meant nothing. Similarly, a therapist tried to encourage Geri by pointing out that ten years earlier Geri could never have imagined herself as being capable of handling her current level of disability.

However, Geri was not concerned with what she had accomplished over the years, but fearful of an uncertain future and depressed over her endless MS.

What these therapists failed to address were the fears, anger and losses felt by their clients. The client has on some level a sense of what she is feeling, and if these very real emotions are ignored, trust and the therapeutic bond is broken. The therapist should never assume that she knows what the client is feeling about her disability. To offer encouragement with the intent of easing the client's pain or avoiding an intense moment focused on the disability is counterproductive; their words may be comforting to a child, but not to a grown woman.

PROBLEM SOLVING

Problem solving for the client is another way the therapist can impose a double bind. While proposing helpful solutions, a therapist may do exactly the opposite. The message she sends is that the client is totally helpless, and incapable of finding solutions to practical problems. One of the goals of therapy is to raise self-esteem by encouraging independence; if the therapist does the thinking for her client it confuses this aspect of therapeutic process. Geri says:

> I have been solving my own problems about my disability for 27 years, so when I explain that I am upset when people hang up on me or don't understand me, I am not asking for solutions. Rather, I am looking for help with my emotional reactions to these frustrating situations. Because I am helpless physically doesn't mean I am helpless intellectually. I have had difficulty communicating for a long time so I know about having other people call for me or writing out what I want to say. I don't know how to deal with my frustration and rage when I am ignored, and I feel ignored when a therapist doesn't listen to my feelings over offering advice.

> Any statement by a therapist which begins with "Why don't you . . . ?" or "Have you tried . . . ?" may be offensive in that it implies the client has not done their best; again, this can be

interpreted as blaming. People who are disabled have lost their motor, visual, auditory, or speech functions and abilities; that does not mean that they cannot think. If a client internalizes these discriminatory messages, they may experience increased feelings of shame, inferiority and worthlessness (Havranek, 1991).

PARTICIPATION IN THE DENIAL OF THE CLIENT

Often people with disability operate in a denial mode, and therapists will aid in this denial. In some ways denial can be very useful to someone who is disabled. It can give them strength that they would not have if they looked at themselves seeing only their disability. Denial enables someone to temporarily disregard their limitations and live as though there were none. Lynn refers to this as her "conscious denial"–what gets her out of bed each morning.

However, too much denial can be harmful; by doing too much the client can become exhausted, ill, or may not ask for help when she needs it because she does not want to admit she is disabled. Without knowing it, the therapist may participate in the denial of the client, thereby creating a bind for the client. Because she wants to show her client that she sees her as a complete person, the therapist may not bring up the subject of disability. To the client stuck in denial, this will reinforce her perceptions that her disability is not acceptable to discuss and that on some level she is not acceptable either. As a result the client could conclude that denying her disability is the appropriate way to function in the world.

As stated earlier, sometimes it is the client who feels tension and discomfort (Comer & Piliavin, 1972) and gives the double message creating a bind for the therapist. At the same time the client says, "Treat me like anyone else," she also says, "Don't forget that I am disabled." If the therapist focuses on the former, the client may feel her disability is being ignored or overlooked. On the other hand, if the disability is given center stage the client will feel she is hardly human. The double bind which the client creates is only a restatement of the way she feels about herself. In other words, she cannot integrate her disability with her desired self-image and still feel whole. The therapist may not wish to think of the client as disabled because she may have similar unexamined issues about disability. With the purest of intentions, she may want to oblige the client in making her feel that she is being treated like a person and not a disability. Again, the message sent is that she is only all right as long as the disability and its related issues are not discussed. With such an enmeshed double bind, the two have no choice but to conspire not to talk about exactly those issues that are most troublesome to the client and possibly to the therapist.

LACK OF DIFFERENTIATION

Similarities as well as differences between therapist and client have a potential for being disruptive to the therapeutic process when they are not recognized and accounted for (Lerman, 1989). As we see from the previous examples, neither the therapist nor the client knows how much focus to give to the disability, but the issue must be addressed in some way. If the therapist spends too much time focusing on the disability, the client will feel reduced to a collection of symptoms. On the other hand, if little time is given to it, the client will feel unheard or dismissed.

There are strong societal norms to treat the person who is disabled either with special care or just like anyone else (Hartsof et al. 1979). A woman who is disabled goes to a therapist because she probably doesn't feel safe talking about her fears, losses, frustrations, or the way she views herself and the world anywhere else. What she does not want is a therapist who ignores their obvious differences, thus impeding the therapeutic process. Overall, it would be a more beneficial tactic for the therapist to acknowledge her client's disability in order to facilitate interaction (Lerman, 1989).

CONCLUDING STATEMENTS

With all of the potential areas where problems can occur, it is a wonder that successful therapy is possible. Yet it does happen. As Geri recalls:

I had been functioning in the world for a long time and people admired me for my independence and perseverance. But I knew there was a problem. It didn't matter that I had a successful long-term relationship with my live-in attendant and his wife, or that I had a job where many people respected me, or that I had a reputation of defiance and resourcefulness. All I know is that I was lonely and depressed much of the time. Also, I had been an insomniac for many years. I felt like a fraud. My neurologist sent me to a young woman psychiatrist in the Sleep Disorders Clinic. Therapy with her was different–more intense than I had experienced before. Although I spoke more of my disability than I had in 27 years, I felt freer of it than I had in a long time. She saw me as a capable, professional woman with a severe disability. I didn't have to overly stress the former so that she wouldn't be uncomfortable by the latter. I felt like a complete person. For the first time I knew I didn't need to hide my true feelings.

There were several things she did that made me feel I was a human being. She touched me–my arm or my shoulder–a simple yet powerfully meaningful gesture. Because someone who uses a wheelchair is surrounded by metal does not mean she is untouchable. One day she wondered aloud what her life would be like if she had multiple sclerosis. The impact was tremendous. It communicated that she thought she and I were not all that different; we were both professional women–not able-bodied and disabled. The therapeutic distance was broken, and with it my isolation. It was the most therapeutic thing she could have done.

As counselors, we find that confrontation and directness combined with a great deal of support is effective. Our own issues with disability are no different than those we have seen counseling others with disability and chronic illness: loss, fear, distorted self-image, anger, and denial. When therapy works, it is because these feelings are addressed and there are no contradictory messages conveyed during the therapeutic process. Therapists treating clients–with or without disability or chronic illness–should accept the client as she is. After all, the most basic premise of good counseling is to be non-judgmental, while at the same time encouraging the growth process. Often a heavy burden is placed on the individual with disability to act in an acceptable way (Comer & Piliavin, 1972). The expectations of the therapist significantly influence the therapeutic process, even more so than the client's expectations (Schofield & Kunce, 1971). Thus, it is the therapist's responsibility not to convey messages of disapproval, or of personal expectations or values. The therapist must acknowledge and examine her own feelings and biases about disability (Lerman, 1989; Schofield & Kunce, 1971), point out the inconsistencies in the client's messages, and interact in a way that communicates she sees the client as whole. Most importantly, the therapist should make sure communications made by both the client and herself are clear and understood, and that every effort is made to act in a non-biased manner when treating the client with disability.

REFERENCES

Asch, A., & Rousso, H. (1985). Therapists with disabilities: Theoretical and clinical issues. *Psychiatry, 48,* 1-12.

Belgrave, F.Z., (1984). The effectiveness of strategies for increasing social interaction with a physically disabled person. *Journal of Applied Social Psychology, 14*(2), 147-161.

Cheever, J., (1991). *The Journals of John Cheever.* New York, Alfred Knopf.

Comer, R., & Piliavin, J.A. (1972) The effects of physical deviance upon face-to-face interaction: The other side. *Journal of Personality and Social Psychology, 23,* 33-39.

Elliot, T.R., MacNair, R.R., Herrick, S.M., Yoder, B., & Byrne, C.A. (1991). Interpersonal reactions to depression and physical disability and dyadic interactions. *Journal of Applied Social Psychology, 21,* 1293-1302.

Fine, M., & Asch, A. (1988). Disability Beyond Stigma: Social Interaction, discrimination, and activism. *Journal of Social Issues, 44,* 3-21.

Hadley, R.G., & Brodwin, M.G., (1988). Language about people with disabilities. *Journal of Counseling and Development, 67,* 147-149.

Hartsof, A.H., Wildfogal, J., & Cassman, T. (1979). Acknowledgment of handicap as a tactic in social interaction. *Journal of Personality and Social Psychology, 37,* 1790-1797.

Havranek, J.E., (1991). The social and individual costs of negative attitudes toward persons with physical disabilities. *Journal of Applied Rehabilitation Counseling, 22*(1), 15-20.

Huitt, K., & Elston, R.R., (1991). Attitudes towards persons with disabilities expressed by professional counselors. *Journal of Applied Rehabilitation Counseling, 22*(2), 42-43.

Lerman, H., (1989). Increasing our sensitivity to the implications of similarities and differences between therapists and clients. *Women & Therapy, 8*(4), 79-92.

Register, C., (1987). *Living with chronic illness: Days of patience and passion.* New York: Free Press.

Schofield, L., & Kunce, J. (1971). Client disability and counselor behavior. *Rehabilitation Counseling Bulletin, 14*, 85-94.

The Prize:
Disability, Parenthood, and Adoption

Jane Zirinsky-Wyatt

SUMMARY. *The Prize: Disability, Parenthood, and Adoption* details the concerns and experiences of the author and her husband, an interracial couple with disabilities, during the process that culminated in the adoption of their daughter. The author discusses the reactions of others–relatives, social workers, doctors, lawyers, friends, and her husband–to her desire to have a child, and reveals her own considerations and fears. She also documents the couple's experiences, good and bad, with fertility doctors, support groups, adoption agencies, and private adoption lawyers. The article should be of special interest to those involved or interested in the adoption process, particularly as it applies to disabled and/or interracial couples.

SUMMER, 1991

The apartment door opens, then slams. Footsteps in the hallway. A small voice, "'Body home? I'm come home awready. Whatcha doin,' Mommy?"

Jane Zirinsky-Wyatt holds an MA in Human Sexuality from New York University, where she has completed all course work for the PhD. She works as a counselor at Barrier-Free Living. Ms. Zirinsky-Wyatt lives in Manhattan with her husband and daughter.

Correspondence may be addressed to: Jane Zirinsky-Wyatt, Two Fifth Avenue, New York, NY 10011-8841.

[Haworth co-indexing entry note]: "The Prize: Disability, Parenthood, and Adoption." Zirinsky-Wyatt, Jane. Co-published simultaneously in *Women & Therapy* (The Haworth Press, Inc.) Vol. 14, No. 3/4, 1993, pp. 43-54; and: *Women with Disabilities: Found Voices* (ed: Mary E. Willmuth, and Lillian Holcomb) The Haworth Press, Inc., 1993, pp. 43-54. Multiple copies of this article/chapter may be purchased from The Haworth Document Delivery Center [1-800-3-HAWORTH; 9:00 a.m. - 5:00 p.m. (EST)].

"Working."
"Workin' de' puter. Find de story, Mommy. Read de story."
"What's the story about?"
"SARA!!!"

I.

Friday, December 30, 1988, 8:30 a.m.–the beginning of the New Year's holiday weekend. The phone rings. I'm getting dressed for work. Chuck is still asleep.

"Hello."

"It's Maris. Did I wake you? There's a baby girl in Bronx Lebanon Hospital. . . . "

"Oh, my God!"

She tells me that, though the three-month-old baby was premature, she apparently is healthy and ready to go home. Maris also says that this baby looks Black. Our first choice was an interracial baby–my husband is Black and I am Caucasian–but I tell her I don't think it matters at all.

I ask for the day to think about it, and Maris says that, as the baby's been there three months, we can have the entire weekend. I hang up the phone. Chuck has awakened and wants to know everything. As soon as I finish, he says, "What's to think about? Call her back. Tell her we'll take the baby."

I do.

Then I call a nursing agency to ask about getting someone to help with infant care. They assure me that they will be able to send someone, but not until after the holiday weekend.

Somehow, I finish getting dressed, have a quick cup of coffee, and leave for work.

Some time in the middle of the day, Chuck calls to say that Maris has called again. When she spoke with the hospital and informed them that she had found a family, they immediately discharged the baby. Maris said she would pick her up at the hospital and bring her to our apartment after work. Chuck reminds me to stop on the way home and pick up a Snugli.

Oh, my God! This is the day I've been waiting for. I'm terrified–I don't know anything about taking care of an infant! Somehow, I make it through the day. Somehow, I make it to Schneider's to buy a

Snugli. Somehow, I manage to drive home. Chuck calls the pharmacy to order diapers and formula. When the delivery man comes, he recognizes us because of his many trips here with fertility medications. "Oho! The twelve hundred dollar prescription!" He grins from ear to ear and demands a cigar.

We are watching TV when the downstairs bell rings and José, the doorman, says "Baby coming up." Then Maris is at the door, holding a tiny bundle wrapped in a blanket. I can't believe it! I look at the bundle, but I'm so nervous that Chuck has to take her.

Maris hands us packages–some formula, and clothes. This tiny person has clearly charmed the hospital staff, for she has come with quite a wardrobe. We go over the immediate care instructions and, in response to her question about sleeping arrangements, we explain that a neighbor has promised to lend us a Port-a-Crib.

We talk about the adoption process, about what will happen next. We learn that, technically, we are only foster parents, and will receive monthly payments from the state until the adoption is final; the stipend might even continue until she reaches adulthood should she fall into certain categories.

We also find out that, while the birth mother has shown no interest in the child for three months, neither has she signed papers to surrender the baby; she could return and attempt to take back the baby. Maris reviews with us the steps we will have to go through before the baby is legally ours.

Now I am completely overwhelmed. None of the things I am being told stay with me. We go over all the details several times. Then Maris remembers that her husband is in the car and says, "I can't stay. Stuart is double parked."

I look at the tiny package. Big black eyes stare back at me. I say, "Her name is Sara."

II.

Sara is a joy! She is an easy baby, who almost never cries. It's a good thing, too, because Mommy has absolutely no idea what she is doing.

By the end of the first weekend, I am feeling seriously sleep-deprived. Sara weighs just five pounds, two ounces, and needs to be fed every two and a half hours. I suspect that what saved my life–or at least my sanity–was being married to a man who has lots of experience with children, and almost never panics. He also watches television until all hours of the night, so he took care of all the really late feedings until she slept through the night.

Sunday is New Year's Day. Traditionally, this is the one day of the year on which Chuck and I entertain. It's nothing fancy–Chuck makes eggnog, I make dip, we serve cheese and crackers. Everybody seems to have fun. This year will be Sara's debut.

Chuck takes care of the last-minute shopping, so that I can stay with Sara. My mother is convinced that we cannot have people over this weekend, that nobody can touch Sara. Nevertheless, we are anxious to show off our belated holiday present so we go ahead with our plans.

Some of our guests know about Sara, and they bring gifts. Some we haven't had a chance to call, and they don't know–I think they are embarrassed. I am too excited and too tired to care. Everybody loves our daughter. Everybody fusses over her. I am thrilled!

The next morning, our adoption attorney calls. He has heard from a birth mother in Missouri with whom we had spoken several months ago. Since she hadn't gotten back to us, we had long since assumed that she had made other plans. Over the holiday weekend, she has given birth to an interracial baby boy. I am exhausted. "Michael, I don't think I can handle *two!*" "If you take the boy, you might have to give Sara back." I don't even have to think about it. "Michael, Sara's home. Sara stays."

III.

Although I had grown up disabled–I was born with cerebral palsy–I had always walked, albeit somewhat slowly and awkwardly, always lived in the mainstream, and I often lived with the illusion that I was "passing." However, I had disabled friends, a sense of disability as a political issue and I even had gotten involved in wheelchair sports. I had made the startling discovery that, far from being the prison we had been taught to fear while living in the able-bodied world, a wheelchair could be a useful tool. Using a lightweight chair enabled me to enjoy museums, to participate in sports, and–as I later discovered–to carry thirty pounds of toddler without losing my balance.

One weekend, I went to a track and field meet in Pennsylvania. On Saturday night, while with some friends from a New Jersey team, I found myself flirting with a bright, witty, handsome guy who played and coached wheelchair basketball. We talked until all hours of the morning, and we even exchanged telephone numbers, but I really didn't expect to hear from him.

Lo and behold, he called that very week, and we made a date. It was a weekday evening, and we had planned for him to come over, stay just a little while, talk, maybe have a snack. As it turned out, he got lost and arrived very late. We talked for a while, then I, the perfect hostess, proceeded to fall asleep. He let himself out. I figured that was the end of the relationship, but he called the next day.

By the second date, I knew that I was falling for Chuck. About this time, he made it clear that he was not interested in marriage, and had no plans for children. Employed as a sex educator in a sheltered workshop and trying to write a dissertation at the same time, I was not at all concerned with permanent commitment. But I knew I was falling in love.

By the time Chuck chose to tell me he had kidney failure, I knew that I could handle the other aspects of his disability, but I didn't know if I could deal with what I saw as a death sentence. It was a devastating experience, but we continued to see each other every weekend.

We went on like this for a long time. I swore I'd never do it, but I did. I loved this man. I adored this man. And I guess I preferred his terms–no involvement, no plans–to losing him. I had dated a lot. I knew what was out there, and I knew I preferred what I had to what I saw around me.

But then something happened. I began to hear my biological clock ticking. I had never thought much about motherhood, on a conscious level. I think it was because I never really thought anyone would marry me. In the sixties, when I was in my twenties, educated, middle-class white women didn't have babies without husbands. They had abortions. In the seventies, I had one myself.

But now we were in the eighties when, faced with a biological deadline, some women were deciding that having a baby was more urgent than having a husband. I joined a support group called Single Mothers by Choice and stopped using birth control. I didn't really

expect anything to happen right away–Chuck's medical history did
not bode well for fertility and, because of a problem unrelated to my
cerebral palsy, neither did mine. I thought that if anything happened, we'd deal with it, and if nothing happened, we'd talk about
it. Nothing happened, and we talked about it.

What I found out was that, while I was ready to consider a baby
without marriage, Chuck wasn't. Two of his brothers had had children that way, and he was quite unwilling to do so. But he was
willing to go to the doctor with me, and we went.

The first fertility doctor we saw was very uncomfortable with us,
but not because of our marital status or our disabilities. She had
dealt with unmarried women before–in fact, the friend who referred
me was unmarried–but she was ill at ease because we were an
interracial couple. She simply couldn't fathom why any White
woman would want a Black child, for any reason, under any circumstances. Although she was always polite, she treated us for only
a few months, then referred us to someone who was more understanding.

While all this was going on, something else happened–Chuck
asked me to marry him! Apparently, he had been thinking about it
and planning it for quite some time, but it came as a total shock to
me. In fact, when he asked me I was so surprised that I lost my
balance and landed on my behind. But then I figured that if I didn't
hurry up and answer him, he might change his mind–so I said yes.
We became engaged in November of 1986, and were married in
May of 1987.

IV.

As we continued our fertility quest, we began to explore the
adoption option.

In the fall of 1987, we attended our first meeting of the Adoptive
Parents' Committee, a support group. We met an attorney and a
social worker who felt they could help us. To be sure, just as at the
single mothers' group, there were some people who were shocked
or uncomfortable with the idea of us as parents, but we were never
quite sure why. For the most part they shied away, so we couldn't
know whether the issue was race, disability, or simply personality.
On the other hand, friends with disabilities had preceded us here,

and most of the people in the group understood that disabilities did not have to preclude adoption. Our status as an interracial couple was not disturbing to them either; several of the Caucasian couples had already adopted interracial or Asian babies.

We had support outside the group, too, sometimes from unexpected sources. At about the time I joined the Single Mothers' group–prior to Chuck's proposal–my mother said to me at lunch one day, out of the clear blue sky, "I think you should adopt a baby." When I said, "Actually, I've been thinking about having a baby," I thought she was going to fall in the soup! It turned out, though, that the idea of my becoming a single mother didn't particularly faze her. Rather, she was concerned about my ability to survive a pregnancy, especially in light of the problem that had created my infertility.

Another source of support was my grandmother, then in her late eighties, retired, and living in Florida. She had no great-grandchildren. On that year's trip to New York to visit, we spoke. It seemed to her that our adopting would complete a circle. When my grandfather came to this country, he spent his early years in an orphanage for Jewish children. In addition, she revealed to me that one of her sisters had two adopted children, close in age to my mother. She was all for the adoption–after all, it was family tradition.

Once we began to consider adoption, it seemed quite logical. I had never really had issues about whether my child came from my womb. To me, motherhood was about a relationship between two people. And, although many men are reluctant to adopt because they feel it an affront to their masculinity, Chuck seemed to have no such problem. Probably one of the reasons I pursued fertility treatments for as long as I did was that I could not believe that anyone would allow us to adopt–my perception was that agencies would see me as unable to care for myself, let alone for a child.

We did have one advantage, though. Everyone talks about a shortage of children to adopt when what they really mean is that it often seems difficult to find a white newborn. We didn't have that problem because we weren't looking for that baby.

I had a graduate school friend who was working in a New Jersey agency. While she did not work specifically in adoption, she knew that they were always looking for interracial couples who were stable and financially secure. She asked if they would consider a couple in which both partners were disabled, and was told that we should call for an interview.

We made an appointment and went to their office, not once but twice. We were interviewed by two different social workers who seemed very impressed with us. They did say that we would have to submit letters from our own doctors, and that the final decision would rest with their medical board. However, they did not appear to feel that there would be a major problem. They sent us home with a lot of forms to fill out. We were very encouraged.

My internist was very supportive, and wrote a letter right away. Chuck's doctor was a little reticent—he was afraid that if he were honest about all of Chuck's medical issues, we would not be considered. I suggested to him that I would draft a letter, and he could then edit it and have it typed on letterhead.

Now we would have to find a New Jersey address, and we set about looking for an apartment in New Jersey but near New York City. After a lot of searching, we found a beautiful new condominium building in Jersey City. I was very ambivalent. I had lived alone in Manhattan since 1970, knew my way around, and had a system of survival that worked for me. But, I thought, if we have a chance for a baby in New Jersey . . . so, we signed a lease. I figured this was an acceptable compromise—we would have the option to buy the apartment at the end of the lease, and if we were really miserable, we could always move back to Manhattan at that time. We ordered new bedroom furniture.

The day the furniture arrived I was elated. I called the adoption agency that morning with the intention of making an appointment to begin the home study process, and left a message for the social worker. When she called me back, she was very curt. "I don't know why you're calling me. Everything is in the letter." I was confused. "What letter? I'm calling because I haven't heard from you." "Oh," she said, "you were rejected." She didn't want to stay on the phone. After we ascertained that the letter had been misaddressed, this professional social worker had nothing more to say to me.

I hung up the phone and I lost it. I called Chuck at the New York number, informed him what had happened, and I told him I needed him to come over right away. I couldn't stop crying—I had given up

Manhattan, left what I knew and loved, for nothing. My hopes had been raised and ruined. I was so hurt.

The letter that eventually arrived stated that the medical board had determined that "the severity of both of your conditions was such that to place an infant in your care would present extensive risk to the overall best interest of the child." This decision was made by physicians who had never laid eyes on either of us! It was also made without any consideration of our financial resources, which easily could have covered the cost of live-in care had they recommended it.

We needed, at that point, to reevaluate our options. Private adoption–adoption arranged without an agency–is easier in New York than in New Jersey. And we already had an adoption lawyer in New York. We had also just found Family Focus, an agency that places a lot of hard-to-place kids in New York City. In New Jersey, we had nothing except a two-year lease on an apartment into which I could hardly stand to set foot.

This was really one of the few times in my life I was thankful for my family's financial means. If we played our cards right, we could keep our rent-stabilized apartment in New York and meet the rent on the condominium, at least until we decided what to do next. And that is what we did. Since my job is in New York, we spent most of the week at the apartment there, but on the weekends, we often went to the condominium. This went on for nearly two years.

As the lease on the New Jersey apartment came close to term, we began a serious search in our Manhattan neighborhood. We found a beautiful apartment right near Washington Square Park that had a bedroom for Sara, and a room we could use for an office. We bought it.

In the meantime, the social worker in private practice who had done our original home study had become a consultant to Family Focus. She updated the study and submitted it to the agency. Maris assured us that we were accepted.

This all happened in the fall of 1988. Nevertheless, we were still looking for a private adoption. We had ads running in several newspapers and twice had the experience of a birth mother who agreed to surrender her baby to us, only to change her mind. We were lucky–

in neither case did we actually see the baby. Still, we were strung out, depressed, and frustrated as the holidays approached.

Over Thanksgiving weekend, we were contacted by a woman who claimed that she had given birth to twin girls. However, before we could decide whether or not to proceed, we discovered that no such person was in the hospital in which she claimed to be, nor had any twins been delivered over the weekend.

It was in this context that Sara came into our lives at New Year's. After the holiday weekend, after she had come to live with us, we received the medical reports about her birth. I know that, had I seen the papers prior to Sara's arrival, I never would have taken her into my home. She had no prenatal care. Her birth mother had been using street drugs. Her birth weight was only thirty ounces–under two pounds!

I have come to the conclusion that being born after only 27 to 28 weeks' gestation may in fact have been Sara's salvation. Had she been a full-term baby, she might have left the hospital with her birth mother after two or three days. She also would have had ten to thirteen more weeks of drug exposure, and she probably would not have had exchange transfusions.

After Sara arrived, we had her checked out by a pediatrician. The doctor was everything I wanted: reassuring, not condescending, really good with kids, and not afraid of educated interracial parents with disabilities. He was very thorough and very reassuring. On the whole, he felt she was healthy and said, "By a year, she'll be all caught up." I remember it verbatim, because I laughed–I didn't believe him. He was right.

VI.

I needed to learn about childcare–I had never handled a baby before. In the beginning, I was afraid. But I gained confidence as I handled my daughter; she adapted, too. Chuck says that, very early, she knew the difference between being picked up by me and being picked up by him or the baby sitter–she would help me by the way she shifted her weight. I also had to experiment with different kinds of carriers before I found one that worked for me.

One thing surprised me. I had expected that I would spend a lot more time in the wheelchair once I had a baby, but it didn't turn out that way at first. When she was really little we were still in the studio apartment, a small place, and I was able to carry her more than I expected. When I couldn't carry her, I used the stroller, even in the apartment.

It was when she was really walking and running that I started spending a lot more time in the chair. That's really the way she knows Mommy, but she's also learned to wear her strap and adapt her pace to mine, whether I'm walking or using the chair.

Sara turned three in October, 1991. In July of 1991, the agency went to court to terminate the rights of the birth mother. After that, the state requires a minimum wait of ninety days before finalization. Meanwhile, as we wait, Sara is the light of our lives! She is a bright, verbal child who loves animals, music, red cars, and strawberry ice cream cones. Although she doesn't yet know what the word "adoption" means, she has heard, many times, the story of how Maris brought her home in a yellow blanket. And we live for the day when a gavel will sound, and when she will finally, legally, be our daughter.

POSTSCRIPT, THURSDAY, JULY 2, 1992

As befits July in New York, it is a hot, muggy morning. We arrive early at the courthouse. We wait. Finally ushered into the judge's chambers, we are such a crowd that the judge asks that we identify ourselves for the record: two grandmothers, two uncles, Sara's beloved babysitter "Viwet"–Violet, Maris, our attorney, two nervous parents, and a tall, self-possessed three-year-old girl in a light blue dress. When asked, she tells the judge "I'm named Sara Jordan Wyatt" and that she lives "in New York City."

The procedure is brief, maybe thirty minutes. It mainly consists of our identifying our own previously notarized signatures on a slew of documents. "Is this your signature?" "I guess so." Would I recognize a good forgery?

Chuck and I hold hands. I have tears in my eyes. The whole thing is vastly anticlimactic. When it is over, we go with both grandmas to eat in Chinatown.

Sara is unimpressed. She wants to know why the judge did not sit behind a high table "like onna teevee," and "where is de gavel, Mom?"

When we tell her that, at last, she is adopted, she looks exasperated, as if these grown-ups have got it all wrong. "I'm adopted *awready,* Mom!"

Women Who Are Visually Impaired
or Blind as Psychotherapy Clients:
A Personal and Professional Perspective

Mary Harsh

SUMMARY. Women who are visually impaired or blind may face specific stressors related to their physical limitations in addition to the stressors that those who are not physically limited face. Several factors may limit this population's utilization of mental health services including problems with mobility, accessibility of mental health professionals, and attitudes about visual impairment and blindness from both the client and the therapist. Psychotherapists need to acquire knowledge about the various types of visual impairment; the impact these impairments have on daily functioning; and the interactions of these impairments with societal demands to become more effective in working with this population. In addition, therapists need to explore their attitudes about visual impairment and blindness. Historically, blindness has been one of the most feared disabilities. This paper contains practical guidelines for working with women who are visually impaired or blind derived from personal experience as a psychotherapy client, from work as a rehabilitation specialist for the blind and visually impaired, and from work as a student-therapist who is partially sighted.

Mary Harsh is a Blind Rehabilitation Specialist and a doctoral candidate in clinical psychology.

Correspondence may be addressed to: Mary J. Harsh, W.B.R.C.-124, DVAMC, 3801 Miranda Avenue, Palo Alto, CA 94304.

[Haworth co-indexing entry note]: "Women Who Are Visually Impaired or Blind as Psychotherapy Clients: A Personal and Professional Perspective." Harsh, Mary. Co-published simultaneously in *Women & Therapy* (The Haworth Press, Inc.) Vol. 14, No. 3/4, 1993, pp. 55-64; and: *Women with Disabilities: Found Voices* (ed: Mary E. Willmuth, and Lillian Holcomb) The Haworth Press, Inc., 1993, pp. 55-64. Multiple copies of this article/chapter may be purchased from The Haworth Document Delivery Center [1-800-3-HAWORTH; 9:00 a.m. - 5:00 p.m. (EST)].

55

Women who are visually impaired or blind may face specific stressors related to their physical limitations in addition to the stressors that those who are not physically challenged face. Several factors may limit this population's utilization of mental health services including problems with mobility, accessibility of mental health professionals, and attitudes about visual impairment and blindness from both the client and the therapist.

This paper presents practical guidelines for working in psychotherapy with clients who are partially sighted or blind. This information is derived from my work as a rehabilitation specialist for the visually impaired and blind, from my personal experience as a psychotherapy client who is visually impaired, and from my work in a doctoral program in clinical psychology as a student-therapist who is partially sighted.

PRACTICAL CONSIDERATIONS

Seeking psychotherapy is often a difficult process. When the client is visually impaired or blind, the process can become significantly more difficult. The following is a discussion of practical considerations to be aware of when working with women who are both partially sighted and blind.

Mobility and Office Location

The woman who is visually impaired faces her first potential obstacle to entering therapy when she must physically get to the therapists' office. This first step may be insurmountable depending upon both the woman's mobility skills and the location of the office. These two issues need to be addressed in the initial phone contact.

One's ability to travel independently is not determined by the amount of remaining vision. A woman who is partially sighted could conceivably have more difficulty with mobility than a woman who is totally blind. This could be true for several reasons: (1) the woman who is partially sighted may not use her residual vision efficiently, (2) the woman who is partially sighted may deny how much her vision loss has affected her ability to move about safely,

(3) the woman who is partially sighted may be so frightened or anxious about going out on her own that she is unable or unwilling to go someplace new, and (4) the woman who is partially sighted may be significantly affected by changes in lighting (i.e., daylight, shadows, dusk, cloud-cover, and darkness). Intuitively, the therapist might think that the best time of day to arrange an appointment with a woman who is partially sighted is during daylight. This is true not only because it will probably facilitate the use of her remaining vision, but also because this will prevent her from having to be out walking alone at night. However, there are people who are visually impaired who are so impacted by photophobia (sensitivity to light) that an evening hour appointment would be preferable. A good match between therapist and client may initially be determined by the flexibility in the therapists' schedule and the mobility needs of the client.

The woman who is blind may be impacted by several other factors pertaining to her ability to get to the therapists' office: whether the woman has received formalized mobility training (i.e., from an Orientation and Mobility Specialist, available in most communities), (2) whether the woman has natural orientation skills, and (3) whether she is frightened or anxious about going out on her own to the point that she is unable or unwilling to go someplace new.

The fear or anxiety a woman who is visually impaired or blind may feel about traveling alone warrants additional comment. The possibility of violence or attack is an issue that all women must deal with when going out alone. Although there are no large-scale studies of women who are blind or visually impaired in relation to this issue, one may easily see how this group of women are at increased risk for violence or attack. Several factors make this group more vulnerable. Many women who are visually impaired or blind need to use a white cane, guide dog, or assistance from individuals with full vision because of their limitations in mobility. These assistive devices and techniques also signal to those around them that they have physical limitations. Their visual limitation also decreases their ability to discern when danger is present. They may not be able to take note that they are being watched or followed, and then to seek assistance. Finally, women who are blind or visually impaired generally must rely on public transportation such as buses and taxis.

Use of these forms of transportation often require waiting alone for long periods, and walking to and from bus stops. All of these factors may make women who are visually impaired or blind more vulnerable targets to perpetrators of crime.

Regardless of how well the woman who is visually limited or blind travels, the first time she travels to someplace new she is likely to elicit significant apprehension, uneasiness, and/or fear. These feelings can be assuaged by a therapist who is sensitive to these unique issues. During the first phone contact, the therapist needs to give thorough and explicit directions to the office location. Generally, the woman will be traveling by public transportation (i.e., bus or taxi). Beyond basic information about major cross-streets and street numbers, detailed descriptions of the area are often useful or necessary. These details may include size and shape of the building, number of buildings from the nearest cross-street, number of driveways and/or pathways from the nearest cross-street, side of building to enter, location of door, layout of floor plan, and description of waiting area. In addition, the therapist should ask the client if she needs any other information to facilitate travel to the office.

At times, efficient travel skills and detailed descriptions of the office location will not be enough. I was once referred to a therapist who had her office in the local foothills. I was assured by the referring therapist that there was bus service to the area. When I called the transit system, I learned that the one bus for that area made only three trips per day. The logistics made it unfeasible for me to see this therapist.

The First Session

During the first session, several unique issues arise when working with a woman who is visually impaired or blind. The first one involves determining whether the client would like to move into the office independently or whether she needs or wants physical or verbal assistance.

The easiest way to determine the level of assistance the client needs is to ask. The most appropriate way to physically assist a client who is visually impaired is through what is known as 'sighted guide technique.' This technique involves the person who is visually impaired holding onto the arm of the person who is sighted right above the elbow. This position is most helpful because the person who is sighted is a half step in front of the guided person, which allows for advanced warning of turning or elevation changes (i.e., stairs or slopes). Unfortunately, well-intentioned people often automatically grab the arm of the person who is blind to do the guiding. Instead of being helpful, this position can feel as though the person who is visually impaired is being pushed or pulled rather than guided. In addition, it leaves the person who is visually impaired less in control of her own movement and body.

A commonly used question in formalized mobility training is "Would you like to take my arm?" (from the individual who is fully sighted), or "May I take your arm?" (from the individual who is visually impaired or blind). If the answer is yes, the person who is sighted needs only to touch the back of her hand to the hand of the person who is visually impaired. This physical contact will enable the person who is visually impaired to locate the guide's arm. This process can be very natural and quick, and can help to avoid an embarrassing or awkward situation in the first few minutes of the session.

Some therapists may have strong reservations about having physical contact with their clients. Physical contact between therapist and client is a complex clinical and ethical issue that has gained considerable attention in recent years (Holub & Lee, 1990). Physical contact is a very different kind of experience from verbal or visual contact. Touching between therapist and client may lead to misunderstandings or inappropriate behavior, and it may elicit sexual feelings in the therapist or client. Women are at particular risk for sexual exploitation by therapists. Holroyd and Brodsky (1980) found that a higher frequency of erotic physical contact occurs between male therapists and their female clients. In addition, these male therapists advocated nonerotic physical contact only with opposite-sex clients indicating a sexist therapy practice. It may be difficult to determine where nonerotic touching ends and erotic touching begins. Therapists need to remember that the sighted guide technique is an accepted and appropriate method of providing necessary physical assistance to individuals who are visually impaired and blind. However, a discussion of the impact and relevance of touching on the therapeutic relationship is necessary given the complexity of engaging in physical contact with clients.

Once inside the office, information that is helpful will differ depending upon whether the woman is partially sighted or blind. For the client who is blind, it can be useful to describe the layout of the room in terms of size and positioning of the furniture. This may also be helpful to clients who are partially sighted. The client may want to practice moving from the waiting area to the inner office independently, or to review this process verbally. These issues will vary from woman to woman. An awareness of these issues can enhance the therapists' effectiveness and ease in working with women who are visually impaired or blind. In addition, the degree of comfort and familiarity the therapist has with issues relating to sight loss will likely signal an acceptance of the woman and her disability.

Lighting and Distance

Two key elements of the physical environment in the therapists' office can have a profound effect on the comfort level of the client who is partially sighted. Both artificial and natural lighting may impact how well the woman is able to see the therapist, and how physically comfortable the environment feels to her. In addition, the seating arrangement in terms of proximity may impact the communication between therapist and client.

Many people who are visually impaired are affected by glare and lighting/illumination. For example, the glare coming from a window can actually prevent the individual who is partially sighted from seeing the features of another person's face who is positioned in front of the window. The glare can also cause physical discomfort and lead to headaches and/or muscle strain from squinting. For some, even sitting with the window to one's side causes too much discomfort. If closing drapes or blinds does not cut down on enough of the glare, the furniture may need to be arranged so that the client is able to have her back to the window.

Illumination from ceiling lights and table lamps can also impact the comfort level of the client who is partially sighted. People with some types of visual impairments require bright light to enable them to use their residual vision most effectively. Others may need relatively low and indirect lighting to function well visually. Recognition of this important issue, and flexibility on the therapists' part will help to create a more comfortable environment for the woman who is partially sighted. One therapist I saw demonstrated this type of sensitivity. First, she showed an interest and willingness to understand how lighting affected my ability to see. We then explored ways to modify the office environment to make it visually more comfortable for me. This involved shutting blinds and turning off a lamp close to my chair. In addition, she moved her easy chair away from the glare of the window. What I found so impressive was that she remembered to make these changes each week. These actions served to facilitate the building of our rapport during the early stages of therapy more than any other comment or action I can recall.

The physical distance between the client who is partially sighted and the therapist may also affect their communication. However, this is a potentially more difficult issue to resolve. Therapists' styles differ in terms of their desired distance from the client. Their style is based on personal preference and professional training, and they may not feel comfortable modifying this distance. Yet, the therapist and the client may benefit from a discussion concerning how much detail the client is able to see in terms of the therapist's facial features and expressions. A small difference in the distance may determine whether the client is able to discern facial expressions or body gestures from the therapist. With other clients, the distance necessary for meaningful visual contact may be uncomfortably close for the therapist and/or the client. An awareness of this potential limitation in their ability to communicate can help the therapist make adjustments in her style of expression. For example, feelings she may convey entirely through facial or bodily gestures may need to be expressed verbally to enable the client to experience or be aware of these feelings.

As noted above, sometimes the physical distance between the therapist and the client is too large to permit meaningful eye contact during the session. However, the client may be able to have this contact when standing closer to the therapist. This adds to the importance of the initial greeting of the client, and the final moments before the session ends. During these moments, the client who is partially sighted may be able to discern more about the therapist's appearance. This added familiarity may increase the clients' comfort with the therapist.

PSYCHOLOGICAL CONSIDERATIONS

Therapist Issues

Historically, blindness has been one of the most stigmatized and feared disabilities. Although treatment of the blind and visually impaired has improved, negative attitudes and irrational beliefs about blindness still exist. Recently, I was confronted with such an attitude in a doctoral-level course in clinical psychology. After class one evening, I had a private discussion with the professor describing the difficulty I have in group discussions because I am unable to see facial expressions. He encouraged me to explain the situation to the class the following week. When I did so, one woman in the class exclaimed "Hmmm, you look like a normal person!" She had been unaware that I am partially sighted. Now I was in some way not "normal" in her eyes.

Being 'differently-abled' by a visual impairment or blindness is often viewed as being not normal. Unfortunately, being 'not normal' usually carries a negative stigma as opposed to being seen as unique. Therapists need to explore their beliefs about what it means to be visually impaired or blind before and during their work with this population.

It is tempting for therapists to assume that the primary issues brought to therapy by women with visual impairments will center around sight loss. In actuality, the range of issues brought to therapy by women who are visually impaired are as diverse as those presented by women who are fully sighted. Therapists need to be alert for any tendency on their part to over emphasize sight loss as an issue.

Client Issues

Loss of vision may not be the major reason a woman with a visual impairment seeks psychotherapy. However, the challenges of living in a visually oriented world can influence many of the concerns typically brought to therapy. The issue of independence versus dependence provides an example.

Regardless of how independent a woman who is partially sighted or blind is, or may want to be, she must still rely on others for help with some aspects of her daily life. This assistance may come in the form of rides to work or to run errands, or help with reviewing her mail. A woman who is visually impaired with a strong need to be in control may find it difficult to accept any help or support for these necessary tasks. This rejection of assistance can add to the stress in her life.

On the other hand, a woman who is visually impaired who has a strong dependency need may focus on the real problems caused by her sight loss rather than explore other reasons for the dependency. Therapists who have knowledge of the types of skills a sight impaired person can acquire through rehabilitation training will be better equipped to explore this aspect of the client's coping style.

Vision loss also complicates other aspects of interpersonal relationships. A woman with a visual impairment must cope with being treated differently, and at times thoughtlessly by people who are uncomfortable or unfamiliar with the disability. Simple social interactions can be complicated by the inability to recognize people's faces or accurately identify body language and other nonverbal cues.

The specific manner in which the challenges of visual impairment interact with other personal issues varies greatly among clients. Therapists need to be aware of the challenges faced by women with visual impairments and be willing to explore the nature and degree to which these challenges influence the client's presenting complaint.

CONCLUSION

This paper has presented some of the basic practical and psychological issues that may arise when working with a woman who is visually impaired or blind in psychotherapy. The therapist's knowledge and sensitivity concerning these issues will help to promote a more comfortable and therapeutic environment for both the client and the therapist.

REFERENCES

Holroyd, J. C., & Brodsky, A. (1980). Does touching patients lead to sexual intercourse? *Professional Psychology, 11*(5), 807-811.

Holub, E. A., & Lee, S. S. (1990). Therapists' use of nonerotic physical contact: Ethical concerns. *Professional Psychology: Research and Practice, 21*(2), 115-117.

The Common Agenda
Between Old Women,
Women with Disabilities and All Women

Shevy Healey

SUMMARY. Popular belief assumes a common agenda between old women and women with disabilities. The stereotype is that all old women are disabled and all women with disabilities may as well be old; both groups are stigmatized and marginalized, even in the feminist community.

While the two groups share social invisibility and oppression, they are different in terms of their history, political goals and philosophy. Both groups desire to distance themselves from each other; those who are disabled because they have too often been warehoused into nursing homes with the old, the old who may not be disabled and don't want to face that possibility. Yet there exists compelling common ground as both groups struggle against their oppression.

All women face a dual task: to confront their oppressor as well as their own internalization of that oppression. Since women with multiple oppressions are more sharply confronted with both tasks, they are on the cutting edge of the vital issues all women face. They can there-

---

Shevy Healey, PhD, is a 70 year old retired Clinical Psychologist. Now a lecturer, group facilitator on ageism, and political activist, she is one of the founders of Old Lesbians Organizing for Change (OLOC).

This article is a revised version of a talk originally presented at the Advanced Feminist Therapy Institute, October 24-27, 1991, Berkeley, California.

Correspondence may be addressed to: Shevy Healey, PhD, % Many Happy Returns, 6239 College Ave. # 203, Oakland, CA 94618.

[Haworth co-indexing entry note]: "The Common Agenda Between Old Women, Women with Disabilities and All Women." Healey, Shevy. Co-published simultaneously in *Women & Therapy* (The Haworth Press, Inc.) Vol. 14, No. 3/4, 1993, pp. 65-77; and: *Women with Disabilities: Found Voices* (ed: Mary E. Willmuth, and Lillian Holcomb) The Haworth Press, Inc., 1993, pp. 65-77. Multiple copies of this article/chapter may be purchased from The Haworth Document Delivery Center [1-800-3-HA-WORTH; 9:00 a.m. - 5:00 p.m. (EST)].

fore become the teachers and heroes for all women in the common
struggle for empowerment and freedom.

Popular belief almost automatically assumes that there must exist
a common agenda between women who are old and women who are
disabled. This assumption is based on the stereotypes that, first, *all*
old women are disabled and second, *all* disabled women may as
well be old since both groups are stigmatized and marginalized. I
would like to explore this a bit.

Before doing so, I want to present my credentials. With regard to
disability, I have spent a considerable part of my professional life
working with people who were disabled as a result of multiple sclerosis, a chronic debilitating condition for which there is no known cure
or even an accepted treatment. I worked some with individuals and
couples, but mostly with groups–ranging from the newly diagnosed to
the severely disabled, groups of women, significant others, children,
young people and families. I have also spent considerable time training
and supervising peer counselors who have M.S., have co-authored a
training manual for such peer counselors, as well as training professionals–social workers, psychologists, counselors, MDs, nurses and
physical therapists in how to work most effectively with those who
have M.S. I tell you my credentials only because I feel it would be
presumptuous to speak about people who have disabilities without at
least letting you know that I have had some experience in grappling
with the issues of disability and empowerment.

My credentials to talk about old women are, first, my own age; I
am an old woman who has just turned 70. More importantly, however, is my experience as an activist in helping to organize the First
West Coast Celebration by and for Old Lesbians 60 and over, and as
a founding member of the Steering Committee of the Old Lesbians
Organizing for Change (OLOC), as well as coordinating editor and
co-author of a *Facilitator's Handbook on Confronting Ageism for
Lesbians 60 and Over* (Avery, Denslow, Hathaway, Healey, Heidelbach, Martin, & Riddle, 1992).

The worst fantasy of every old woman is that she will become
disabled and unable to care for herself. On the other hand, the worst
fear of most women who are disabled, is that they will be dumped
with the *old* in that particularly unique for-profit institution, the

nursing "home," designed primarily for the old by the medical/insurance establishment. Feelings of women with severe disabilities toward the old are frequently additionally complicated by envy and anger since they do not believe they will ever live long enough to *be* old, or again, afraid that they might.

There are in addition many important differences in the history and philosophy of both groups (Estes, 1986; Heumann, 1986; Kuhn, 1986; Wallace & Mahoney, 1986). The philosophy of action of the social movement of the disabled which resulted in the Americans with Disabilities Act of 1990 is based on a model closely taken from the civil rights movement. Since most of the social services which people with disabilities use–SSI, Medicaid, attendant services, are state and locally based, political action of this group has always emphasized grass roots, local and state organization. A whole host of counterculture organizations of those with disabilities have sprung up which often use militant and unorthodox ways of calling attention to their struggle.

This is in contrast to the movement of the old, where the primary issues of social security and Medicare have resulted in organization from the top of a large and extensive federal lobby, led by the formidable and conservative mainstream organization, the American Association of Retired Persons.

The disability rights movement has from its inception fought for the integration of the disabled into the mainstream of society, in direct response to the years when segregating young people with disabilities into separate schools and separate homes was the norm (Heumann, 1986). Young people with disabilities are struggling hard, not always successfully, to break out of society's imposed isolation and invisibility, while old people first face such isolation at a time in their lives when they see their options as having shrunk and their power as minimal (Estes, 1986). The most popular and familiar forms of segregation of the old are the many Senior Centers and special developer-designed residential senior communities throughout the country.

The Independent Living Movement, with its focus on independent living based on consumer controlled attendant care, was founded in Berkeley in the 1960s. This alternative model is not yet being seriously addressed by the organizations of the old. Care for the old who are frail and/or disabled is still tied, almost solely, by tradition and current established practices, to that provided by individual family members (the women, of course), or by institutions (Heumann, 1986).

Both groups are among the poorest of the poor. Old women reap the results of a lifetime of sexist inequity at the work place, while all old workers know what it means to be pushed out of jobs to make room for young and less "expensive" workers. A priority for the disabled community is to find jobs for people who are disabled at decent wages. The major struggle of the old, however, is to retain, extend, and increase social security benefits, so that after a life-time of hard work it may be possible to retire without being totally impoverished.

In addition to all of the former differences cited, the ageism and ableism rampant in our society exists in both groups. This frequently makes both groups want to distance themselves from each other: those who are disabled because they have all too often been warehoused into nursing homes with the old, the old who may not be disabled and who don't want to face such a possibility. It does make one ask whether there can, in fact, be a common agenda between old women and women who are disabled. In my view, the answer is yes, for, in truth, the *similarities* between the two groups are compelling, much more than their differences (Wallace & Mahoney, 1986). Both women who are disabled and/or old have to spend a considerable amount of their life's time attending to their bodies and engaging with the medical establishment, suffering most acutely from living in a society with no universal health care coverage. The threat of rationing health services is a real concern to both groups, who have been accused of "costing too much," to the detriment of those more "worthy." Both groups face the haunting specter of a not too distant future in which eligibility for care may be based, not upon need, but upon a hierarchy of citizen desirability. Both share in the problems created by the medicalization of social services and the underallocation and underfunding of these services (De Jong, 1986; Zola, 1986). When old age and disability are viewed as abnormalities rather than normal life conditions, help with daily living becomes available only by "prescription" and within medical settings. And when health care has become a huge for-profit establishment, it is inevitable that its focus is on medication, tranquilization and big brother infantilization (Heumann, 1986).

Both groups suffer from the impatience and the insensitivity prevalent in our society toward chronic illness, chronic frailty, chronic need. We may manage, often dramatically, to rise to the occasion of acute illness, but chronic conditions present a more difficult challenge, particularly since our lives are not lived in community, with built-in support networks. Each woman fears the burden of sole responsibility as caregiver.

Both groups are victimized by inaccessible environments, as well as social violence. We have effectively isolated those who have disabilities, both young and old, from the mainstream of life by the physical inaccessibility of public streets and private housing, and by environmental pollutants that rob all of us of good health and some of us of breath and life. Even with increasing attention being called to the inaccessibility of the environment, and even with the passage of the Americans with Disabilities Act, the issue is still approached in terms of "cost," "preference," "available options," and a helplessness in face of the problems, which results most often in gestures rather than solutions. And I speak here for myself and my own shame of living in a house which is totally wheelchair inaccessible to friends who are disabled!

It is very clear that both groups are marginalized, stereotyped and stigmatized. Both groups are hated and feared as well. The dread of both aging and disability is so pervasive in women as to be phobic. We have all heard someone say, "I'd rather kill myself than be . . . as disabled, frail, old . . . as she is." No one wants to be disabled, no one wants to be old. For a woman, to be either means to be rejected as valuable, to be scorned as "less than," as unproductive by all the standards of productivity set by this consumer society, to be seen as unattractive and asexual, to be almost always considered mentally (as well as physically) inferior, to be thought of as useless since the patriarchy considers women most valuable to the extent that they are ornaments or caretakers, as well as the bearers and rearers of the children.

Both women who have disabilities and/or are old have no status in Western-European mainstream society, and are subject to ridicule and attack. Furthermore, both are blamed individually for their difficulties. If only they had been more prudent in their youth, or more careful of their health, exercised more, been more cautious in their habits, or even more spiritual and more able to resolve their personal issues, then surely they would not have become ill, frail, or impoverished. By framing the situation of both those who are old and/or those who have disabilities in terms of personal responsibility, the attempt is to make social irresponsibility acceptable!

To summarize, then, both groups, those who are old and/or those who are disabled, are subject to very similar stereotypes about themselves and similar forms of institutionalized discrimination in their daily lives, in addition to whatever other discrimination they experience because of sexism, racism, anti-semitism, classism, heterosexism. It is also clear that there is a strong basis between the two groups for bonding and common struggle.

Now, what will it take to create a common bond between these two groups, other groups who face special oppression, and all other women?

Feminism, and the struggle against the sexism in our society was to be the common bond, the common agenda between all women. Yet, today, we are sometimes more aware and focused on the differences that divide us than the common agenda we may have to unite us. The greatest barriers between women are those created by the ableism, ageism, racism, anti-semitism, heterosexism and classism of our society. Just to use those "ism" words, however, does not describe the chasm that exists between women—a chasm which is based on denial, fear, repression, avoidance and objectification, a chasm which directly serves the patriarchy.

All women feel sexist oppression under the patriarchy, but that oppression comes in very many disguises, with varying degree of privilege. Sometimes the fist is in a golden glove, rather than in its crudest form of sexual and physical abuse. Some women feel, because they have a greater degree of personal freedom, generally based upon their class, that they have escaped from the worst of patriarchal oppression. Other women, who have worked hard and have achieved some modicum of personal power, are more comfortable with a focus on personal "choice," to the exclusion of social inequity. Their sometimes unacknowledged desire to distance themselves from those who represent powerlessness is frequently based upon real fear for their own future and their own insecure status. They are resistant, frequently without awareness, to finding a common ground between themselves and those "others," even as they themselves are "other." It feels safer and takes less effort to insulate oneself, to keep one's distance, particularly since we live in a society that is very segregated by class, race, and ethnicity.

But since we are "good" people, many of us genuinely feel the unfairness of ableism, ageism, racism, and all the other "isms" which signal special oppression, and we want to change the way things are. We do *want* to become more inclusive. Yet it seems as though no matter what efforts we may make, or how good our intentions, nothing much seems to happen!

Sadly, it is my belief that nothing much will happen if the basis for our efforts is a desire to be "fair," a desire to *be* and *do* "good." My belief is that only the clearest realization of a strong common agenda between all women based on each woman's strong self-interest will create the kind of compelling drive required to unify us.

It is to this point that I want to direct attention. What, then, constitutes the compelling reason for a common agenda?

All oppressed groups face a dual task: to confront their oppressor and to confront their own internalization of that oppression so that they can change their lives. Both tasks go together and both help to radicalize the individual to change society. Women with multiple oppressions are more sharply confronted with both tasks and therefore are on the absolute cutting edge of the most vital issues that *all* women face. They are forced for their own survival to face issues which others may also need to face but have the luxury to ignore. These women, the old, the poor, women with disabilities, women of color–are not braver, or more heroic. It is simply that the intensity of their oppression puts them on the firing line. They are forced to grapple with concepts and issues which provide the possibility (not the guarantee, mind you) of great personal growth and power. They are becoming our heroes and our teachers.

This is the compelling reason for a common agenda because it is based on mutual and common self interest between all women and women who are old and/or have disabilities, who are women of color, of different ethnicities, or poor, or lesbian.

Let me give some examples.

The issues of independence, dependence and interdependence
are issues that we, as women and as therapists, are in the middle of
all the time. Women for years have been accused of being "too"
needy, "too" dependent. And as an "independent" woman myself,
I must admit there was a time when I bought the whole package. I
didn't want to be a wimp. Particularly as a feminist lesbian, I, and
my sister lesbians, feel a special pride in not being male-identified,
in doing non-traditional tasks, in breaking out of traditional female
roles and not acting or being helpless, in being, in a word, "independent."

But as part of my education as a feminist, I have learned that the
concept of being "too" needy is based on a standard of "need"
which has no objective measure, but has been set by the patriarchy
in which boys and men have had, for the most part, their every need
catered to first by their mothers, and then by their wives, mistresses
and secretaries. Little girls and women, who almost always operate
from a deficit of *getting* enough care, since they've been trained
very early on to be *giving* the care, feel shamed because of their
"neediness," and try to hide and dissimulate those feelings, particularly now, when a "super woman" standard prevails.

However, it was only through my work with women who have
disabilities, and my special contact with women involved with the
disability rights movement was I forced to rethink the whole issue
of independence. I remember feeling a real "click" as I read a letter
by Sandra Aronson (1987), a woman with severe disabilities,
printed in the July/August 1987 issue of *The Disability Rag:*

"Elevators were invented to help able-bodied people get to the
60th floor, and escalators so able-bodied people don't have to climb
stairs . . . rich people routinely hire cooks and maids. So *we* need
more help. So what? By virtue of being human and being alive, I am
entitled to shelter, to food and assistance to make what I have of my
life liveable, decent and fun. We are all entitled–because we exist.
That's the entire qualification."

Because of her physical condition, Sandra Aronson, with one fell
swoop has set up different criteria for what constitutes dependence.
She needs help, knows it, and beyond that, knows that it is not a
source of shame, simply a part of the human condition. Money buys
help all the time, help that is taken for granted by the rich and is a

source of humiliation for the poor! It became clear to her and to other women with disabilities that the essence of independence and personal autonomy does not reside in how much we do for ourselves, but in how much we are able to retain decision making power in our lives. This is the basis for the political struggle for *consumer based* attendant care. Now that I am an old woman, I am deeply grateful that I have had an opportunity to begin the learning of this crucial lesson earlier, thanks to the clarity of women like Sandra Aronson.

Or, to take the example of my friend who lives daily with a severe chronic illness, CFIDS, an acronym for Chronic Fatigue Immune Dysfunction Syndrome. CFIDS is a hidden disability which primarily affects women, and is directly related to the increasing levels of environmental pollution we all experience (Barshay, this volume). Under the greatest personal stress because of her illness, nevertheless, my friend has become the vanguard for all of us every time she raises the issue of holding scent-free meetings, in what should be our common concern and our common struggle to save our planet. Every time she shares, without pulling any punches, her experiences as a chronically ill person, she offers us the opportunity to reexamine some of our own basic values and attitudes about disability, illness, life and death. She confronts the "ongoing denial" and "active unwillingness" of most people to deal with the reality of chronic illness, based on the phenomenon of disbelief and hatred for those things that make us feel powerless and helpless. As therapists, particularly, we have much to gain from confronting these issues directly as they become manifest in our own reactions.

Or to take some examples from my own struggles as an old lesbian. Age is a factor for women throughout our entire lives. We are either too young, afraid of getting old, or we are actually old. Only the old, however, are subject to the systematic stereotyping and discrimination which we now call ageism. Old age has ceased to be a stage of life like any other, with advantages as well as disadvantages. It is the *only* time of life that is seen *only* in terms of its negatives. Ageism so pervades women's entire lives that many have a personal terror about growing old, which means to them being ugly, invisible and powerless. It is no wonder then that women will spend much time and energy in the attempt to fool the clock, to pass for younger, as well as, consciously or not, avoid associating with old women so that the stigma does not rub off on them.

It became clear to me, as I went into my 60s, that without confronting my own internalized ageism it would be impossible for me to live a full and rich old age. In confronting ageism, I contend that all women, old and young, shape a new future for themselves. Freeing ourselves from stereotypic expectations means freeing ourselves to be able to experience our own lives.

One of my greatest tasks has been to check on an ongoing basis my own reality against my ageist expectations. For example, having bought the ageist stereotype that sickness in old age is inevitable, I am being forced to deal with my body and its illnesses in a new way. The initial panic I experience upon any illness, almost no matter how slight, is based on my stereotypic expectation that illness in old age is simply the beginning of the end. After all, what else could possibly be in store for me with each passing year. As I learn, and not just intellectually, that most old women can reasonably expect to live in relatively good health until they die, given our level of technical knowledge, I am coming more and more to rely upon my own *experience* rather than my ageist *expectations.* At the same time, I am beginning to understand better what Barbara Macdonald (1991) meant in *Look Me in the Eye,* when, after being angry at her body for "failing" her as she grew old, by not healing her as she was used to, she says: "Today, gradually, sometimes not easily, I begin to understand that my body is still in charge of my life process and has always been. It is still taking good care of me, but it has always had two jobs: to make sure that I live and to make sure that I die. All my life it has been as busy with my dying as my living" (p. 114).

I am much more in touch with my own vulnerability, the fragility of life itself and the issue of my own dying. This proximity to death has forced many of us old women to look more sharply at our values about life. Women from Oakland, California, whose homes were in the path of the 1992 fire, report a similar experience. When, under orders to evacuate, they actually had to prepare what they would take along with them, a different set of priorities governed their choices from the materialism of every day existence. The endlessly interesting process of life itself, our relationships with people, with nature–all become the treasured moments of our existence rather than the possessions we have accumulated.

I think of how feminism has helped so many of us invent our own lives, as it is now helping me to invent my own aging. Yet ageist stereotypes and women's dread of their own aging prevents our talking together as equals, prevents our open dialogue about what matters to each of us. The ritual respect most of us were expected to give the old when we were growing up I experience now as only a poor mask for disrespect and discounting. With the exception of a few old women who can be looked up to as role models, a device guaranteed to create distance, ageist stereotypes tell us that old women's ideas are irrelevant, out of touch, rigid, and conventional.

Having just turned 70, I don't know what it will be like to be 75 and 80 and 90 and beyond. I don't know now what it may mean later to be disabled, to be frail, to need a great deal of help in order to perform the daily tasks of living. I don't know what my bottom line is. I have heard people say, "If I ever have to use a walker, forget it." ... "If I ever have to use a wheelchair, forget it" ... "If I ever lose the use of my hands, forget it." I have seen people change their bottom line as their life has changed.

I don't know now what my bottom line is. I do know that thinking about what constitutes the core of my existence, the core without which I cannot survive, seems a rich and rewarding endeavor. That task is not so different from what it's always been, perhaps more urgent, more poignant. I do feel better equipped to face it. After all, I have more experience and more free time to do what needs doing: to root myself in the present and in whatever my own process is that moves me to reflect, to observe, to participate, to be. Growing old *does* mean growing.

Sharing our lives is the big payoff that a common agenda can bring–for all of us. We travel to broaden our horizons. Yet right here amongst our own we have a diversity of experience and cultures that can sharpen our vision and enhance our lives. I have focused on women with disabilities and old women, but I am speaking, of course, of all women with multiple oppression. The richness that the experiences of women of color can bring to all of our lives, for example, cannot be measured; these women have managed to survive and triumph over unspeakable oppression while developing a culture and a solidarity that is sustaining.

In watching the Hill-Thomas Hearings no one could help but see how the men on the Hearing Committee and in the Senate, just didn't "get it" about what sexual harassment really is like! We don't want any women not to "get it" about what multiple oppression is really like. We women who are most on the firing line have a special role to play in sensitizing all women about what it means to be truly human, and all women can most achieve that expansion of their human experience by joining with us in our common struggle.

For feminist therapists this is a very special mission. We know how critical it is to help women acknowledge their oppression without internalizing the oppressor's message and becoming simply victims. As we struggle together in friendship, as we confront those "isms" in ourselves and each other, and as we play and love together, we not only enhance and empower ourselves and each other, I do believe in this way we change the world!

REFERENCES

Aronson, S. (1987, July/August). Letters to the editor. *Disability Rag.*

Avery, C., P. Denslow, R. Hathaway, S. Healey, R. Heidelbach, V. Martin, K. Riddle, Editors. (1992). *Facilitator's Handbook: Confronting Ageism, Consciousness Raising for Lesbians 60 and Over.* Houston, TX: Old Lesbian Organizing Committee (OLOC).

Barshay, J. (1993). Another strand of our diversity: some thoughts from a feminist therapist with severe chronic illness. *Women & Therapy, 14(3/4),* special issue on *Women with Disabilities.*

Estes, C. (1986). An organizing framework for a unifying agenda. pp. 2-5. *Toward a Unified Agenda, Proceedings of a National Conference on Disability and Aging.* Edited by C.W. Mahoney, Carroll L. Estes and Judith E. Heumann. San Francisco: Institute for Health & Aging, University of California.

DeJong, G. (1986). Needs of disabled persons. In-home attendant services. pp. 46-56. *Toward a Unified Agenda, Proceedings of a National Conference on Disability and Aging.* Edited by C.W. Mahoney, Carroll L. Estes and Judith E. Heumann. San Francisco: Institute for Health & Aging, University of California.

Heumann, J.E. (1986). The independent living movement; benefits for the elderly. pp. 6-12. *Toward a Unified Agenda, Proceedings of a National Conference on Disability and Aging.* Edited by C.W. Mahoney, Carroll L. Estes and Judith E. Heumann. San Francisco: Institute for Health & Aging, University of California.

Kuhn, M.E. (1986). Making history in a time of change. pp. 13-18. *Toward a*

Unified Agenda, Proceedings of a National Conference on Disability and Aging. Edited by C.W. Mahoney, Carroll L. Estes and Judith E. Heumann. San Francisco: Institute for Health & Aging, University of California.

Macdonald, B. with C. Rich. (1991). *Look me in the eye: Old women aging and ageism.* San Francisco: Spinsters Book Company.

Wallace, S.P. & C.W. Mahoney (1986). Issues in disability and aging: background paper, Appendix p.1-6. *Toward a Unified Agenda, Proceedings of a National Conference on Disability and Aging.* Edited by C.W. Mahoney, Carroll L. Estes and Judith E. Heumann. San Francisco: Institute for Health & Aging, University of California.

Zola, I.K. (1986). The medicalization of aging and disability: problems and prospects. pp. 20-40. *Toward a Unified Agenda, Proceedings of a National Conference on Disability and Aging.* Edited by C.W. Mahoney, Carroll L. Estes and Judith E. Heumann. San Francisco: Institute for Health & Aging, University of California.

Looking Through the Mirror of Disability: Transference and Countertransference Issues with Therapists Who Are Disabled

Alison G. Freeman

SUMMARY. This article attempts to examine issues of transference and countertransference in psychotherapy with therapists and clients with disabilities. Common strengths, defenses and limitations of therapists who are disabled are discussed from both a personal and professional perspective. Transference and countertransference reactions are identified in diagnosis, assessment and treatment planning with particular emphasis on expectational systems, strengths and weaknesses. Typical transference reactions of clients who are disabled are often intensified and may include such feelings as anger, resentment, incompetence and comparison with the disabled therapist. Discussion of typical countertransference reactions include guilt and anger, oversheltering, overidentification, overestimation of abilities and codependency with clients.

This article will present some of the author's impressions of the clinical dynamics of transference and countertransference when the therapist is disabled and is working with clients with disabilities.

Alison Freeman, PhD, is a clinical psychologist in private practice in Northern California, specializing in working with people with hearing impairments and other disabilities.

Correspondence may be addressed to: Alison Freeman, PhD, 15951 Los Gatos Blvd., Suite 5, Los Gatos, CA 95032.

[Haworth co-indexing entry note]: "Looking Through the Mirror of Disability: Transference and Countertransference Issues with Therapists Who Are Disabled." Freeman, Alison G. Co-published simultaneously in Women & Therapy (The Haworth Press, Inc.) Vol. 14, No. 3/4, 1993, pp. 79-90; and: Women with Disabilities: Found Voices (ed: Mary E. Willmuth, and Lillian Holcomb) The Haworth Press, Inc., 1993, pp. 79-90. Multiple copies of this article/chapter may be purchased from The Haworth Document Delivery Center [1-800-3-HAWORTH; 9:00 a.m. - 5:00 p.m. (EST)].

Unique and common therapeutic strengths and areas of weakness that emerge in assessment and treatment will be examined.

When I first entered therapy as a teenager with a hearing impairment, I had a hearing therapist who specialized in working with families of children with hearing impairments. I wondered if she could truly understand my feelings about my hearing loss despite her obvious expertise and empathy. I always wished that I could have had a therapist who was also hearing impaired. Later, with subsequent hearing therapists, I found myself experiencing contradictory feelings regarding this difference: irritation at having to teach them about my disability at one extreme and a feeling of specialness in my unique status as a disabled overachiever. Subsequently, in graduate schools and during the last 12 years as a clinical therapist, I have been interested in the unique clinical dynamics when a therapist or client has a disability.

My professional experience with clients who are disabled has taught me that there are variations on the conventional themes of transference and countertransference that are not taught in graduate school. Because most graduate programs still do not offer any specialized training in working with disabled populations, we therapists with disabilities must frequently make expedient modifications and adjustments in our clinical interventions as we go along. In many cases, I openly communicate about my disability and use it as a metaphor for the very communication which serves as the foundation of psychotherapy.

Transferential and countertransferential responses can complicate and obstruct the therapeutic relationship. Regardless of therapeutic modality and style, every therapist with a disability must be prepared to recognize transference and countertransference phenomena as they occur and to determine how to use the information (Gakis, 1990). Awareness and identification of these phenomena are an essential part of our therapeutic responsibility. In turn, this knowledge facilitates accurate interpretation and helps us in our clinical determination of its appropriateness or usefulness to the client.

Transferential and countertransferential issues related to a therapist's disability often arise in the first session. According to Asch and Rousso (1985), a client's initial reactions to the therapist's disability may offer crucial diagnostic clues. For example, some clients may react with feelings of anxiety and fear that the disabled therapist may not be able to meet their needs or handle their anger. Conversely, some clients may feel inspired or hopeful if they know that their therapist has overcome great barriers and that she herself can do the same. Other clients may look at the differences between themselves and their "damaged" therapist who reminds them of their own "damaged" self and feelings of vulnerability. Another less common reaction is to view the disability as merely incidental and not presenting particularly unique problems. Clients who attempt to help their therapist without asking whether help is, in fact, needed may diagnostically indicate caretaking and codependency issues. In any case, the issue of disability must be addressed directly in order to effectively establish the initial therapeutic relationship.

A FEMINIST PERSPECTIVE

A feminist perspective adds to the traditional view of transference and countertransference by highlighting the real relationship between the therapist and client. Eichenbaum and Orbach (1983) stress that as women, we have been exposed to similar societal influences and because of these shared experiences, we, as therapists, will inevitably find many points of identification with our clients. While many resonances of past relationships will be worked on and used in the therapy, there is also a new and real relationship that develops between the woman client with a disability and her therapist. Eichenbaum and Orbach (1983) succinctly state that as therapists, ". . .we listen again and again to the stories of our lives–lives of oppression, compromise, disappointment, frustration, unexpressed rage and staggering bravery. We see again and again how much of this pain stems from the sexual arrangements within patriarchy. . . ." As such, society becomes a critically important paradigm to further understand how transference and countertransference may frequently occur outside and beyond the traditional therapist-client relationship.

Discovery of new role models is often a major curative factor for many women clients with disabilities as they may for the first time see a successful, woman therapist with a disability achieve what they have previously thought impossible. It may well be the first time that the disabled female client has received help from a female, disabled role model. This can be especially healing in cases where the client's mother has been unavailable or unable to help because of her own feelings of helplessness or victimization.

The importance of identification from a feminist perspective is illustrated in the following example which remains vivid in my mind. Jenny, a woman with a hearing impairment, was depressed and voluntarily admitted herself into the hospital during the process of her coming out as a lesbian. The hospital psychiatrist advised her to work harder at being a better mother and wife, and that her lack of conformity was the reason for her depression. Further, he told her that her hearing loss was psychological and that she could really hear if she tried harder. During the intake session with me, she was guarded, fearful and frequently questioned my feelings about homophobia and disability. Understandably, her fear and suspiciousness were justified. Countertransferentially, I was very aware of my own anger towards the psychiatrist and the archaic system that continues to exist today in perpetuating erroneous stereotypes. After a few sessions, when she was able to see that my feminist views were different from those of the hospital psychiatrist and her ex-husband, she relaxed considerably and was able to work on her presenting issues which included her feelings about her hearing impairment.

NATURE OF THE DISABILITY

The nature of the client's disability may have an effect on transference and countertransference by virtue of whether it is considered a temporary or a permanent one, or one that is similar or dissimilar. The client who comes into or becomes temporarily disabled during the process of therapy may experience some guilt or may minimize their own disability if the therapist's disability is a long-standing and permanent one. In a similar vein for therapists, a client's temporary disability may bring up grief issues, and in particular highlight unfinished grieving. Many believe that if someone is born with a disability, there is nothing to mourn since they never had the particular faculty to begin with. However, subjected to non-disabled people asking questions about their limitations, they may still experience the frustration of being limited even though they may not have an exact taste of what it is that they are missing.

The similarity of the client's disability to the therapist's own may also serve as a point of identification or resistance. For example, Bobbi was severely depressed, paranoid and abusing alcohol when she came into therapy with a three year old diagnosis of multiple sclerosis. She had shied away from therapy because of previous treatment by a male psychiatrist who had ignored critical incest and abuse issues. Like many psychiatrists or medical professionals trained in the medical model, he prescribed antipsychotic medication to help her with her paranoia and alcohol abuse without exploring the underlying social and cultural causes. Understandably, she was distrustful of entering into another therapy relationship. Brought in resistantly by a concerned friend, she stated at the end of the session that she thought she could be comfortable with me because I was a woman with a disability who could understand and validate her pain. This identification despite the differences in our disabilities still remains a strong factor in her therapy.

Other clients with differing disabilities will not be able to identify with the therapist's disability. It becomes the therapist's job to evaluate whether this lack of identification is an issue of the client's therapeutic resistance or whether it may be due to the therapist's lack of knowledge about the disability. The following case illustrates this dilemma and how I concluded that this was a case of resistance rather than my lack of knowledge. Susan had an environmental disability and spent considerable time focusing on how her disability was more disabling and different than mine. Susan was referred to me by her previous therapist with a mobility disability who also reported this similar reaction. Critical of both her previous therapist and myself, Susan would frequently express her frustration about my not appreciating the limitations of her disability when we explored possibilities and solutions to her presenting problems. Countertransferentially, I was aware of my own frustration and feelings of "not being a good-enough therapist" despite consultation with therapists who had more expertise with this disability. This case illustrates that although it may be appropriate to interpret certain dynamics as being indicative of resistance, we must also be responsible in educating ourselves about disabilities which we may know little about.

Clients may be in different stages of dealing with their disability. Some may have just started to grapple with the impact of a new identity whereas other clients may be at a point where the disability is not the presenting problem especially if they have already worked on the issue with another therapist. In the beginning stage, the transference may be particularly intense because of identification and a thirst for knowledge and validation. As the therapy progresses, the effects of disability upon the transference may diminish as issues of disability are worked through in the therapeutic process.

TRANSFERENCE

Transference refers to the displacement of feelings and emotional responses from past, childhood figures onto present day relationships and situations (Malan, 1979). Transference with clients who are disabled may be more intense, emotional or sexualized and may center around the shared disability. In the initial phases of traditional psychotherapy, and in most brief therapies, the similarities and differences between client and therapist play an important role in bridging the realities of everyday life and facilitating insight (Hall & Malony, 1983; Schwartz, 1989). The transference becomes more narrow for women as a second similarity of disability is added. In this situation, positive or negative transference may be more intensely experienced. Schwartz (1989) points out that for clients who belong to a minority, the selection of a therapist who belongs to a similar minority(ies) can foster greater acceptance, understanding and growth. However, for other clients who devalue themselves based on their minority status, such a similarity could be a barrier to the therapeutic alliance.

It is also possible that the female client who is disabled may be angry or resentful toward a therapist who is disabled because she herself has overcome barriers of prejudice as a woman and as a person with a disability. At times, there may be a fine line between refusing to collude with the client's sense of victimization and the setting of realistic boundaries and expectations. The attitude of "I did it, so can you" can be helpful if the expectations are realistic but can be distressing or cruel when the client doesn't have the ego strength or the emotional/physical support systems. In these cases, it is more helpful to help the client define goals more realistic to their particular situation.

For example, I have been working on a long-term basis with a 50 year old woman, Marie, who is deaf. Twice-divorced and widowed once, she has experienced an extraordinary amount of childhood abuse and she carried into her adult years a script of being horribly damaged. She has never worked and had no goals in life. She believed her deafness made her incapable and inadequate. She was initially excited about seeing me as a successful deaf woman/therapist with a similar hearing loss. However, she quickly distanced herself because of other factors such as age, social and educational differences. She attended a function where I was being honored as a "Deaf Woman of the Year" and saw my parents and husband in the audience. Thereafter, she would use this difference to reinforce her belief system, to explain how she could never achieve anything and to assert that I had no right to have any expectations of her because "I had been born with an Oneida spoon in my mouth." She concluded that I could not truly understand her nor help her because I came from a privileged background and had a supportive family. In this case, she perceived our social differences to be too great and insurmountable. Although our hearing loss might have served as a juncture, in reality it proved to be more disconcerting than helpful as other differences were worked through.

Another case illustrates an example of the intense process of transference that occurs in a small disabled community. Jane was a 20 year old deaf lesbian in college who was introduced to me by a mutual friend in a semi-social setting. She had a history of extensive childhood abuse resulting in a number of temporary foster placements until she left for college. Deaf since early childhood, she met her first person who was deaf when she was 17 years old and quickly became involved with the deaf community. She entered therapy with me because she wanted to examine her new deaf identity with a hearing impaired, woman therapist as she had been in therapy with several hearing therapists who were men. She developed a very quick rapport with me and surprised herself with the intensity of feelings that she had with me. Transferentially, I became her mother, lover, friend, and teacher, all of which we explored in therapy. Likewise, countertransferentially, I experienced feelings that were substantially more intense than with other clients.

A year later, she found out through the deaf grapevine that I was getting married. She reacted dramatically with fury, disappointment and jealousy and threatened to quit therapy. She was disappointed that I had not told her myself and that she had not been invited to the wedding. Her response, while inappropriate and atypical, is better understood when we look at the deaf community as a family system where interpersonal dynamics are examined with fishbowl intensity and transcend beyond typical boundaries of psychotherapy.

COUNTERTRANSFERENCE

The term countertransference refers to a therapist's conscious or unconscious emotional reactions to the client (DeWald, 1969; Schwartz, 1978). The concept of countertransference may also include responses that may be realistic yet countertherapeutic. Countertransference can be an extremely useful tool if it is recognized and carefully used in diagnosis and treatment (Masterson, 1983).

Countertransference can be described as having two components: (1) the clinician's possibly irrational or inappropriate response to a client's behavior and (2) the way in which a client's configuration of behavior or transference provoked or sparked the countertransferential reaction (Rhodes, 1979). Thus, countertransference can tell us about the undisclosed and unconscious processes in both the therapist and the client. "Getting stuck" may signify areas of unfinished business for ourselves as therapists. Unrecognized, they may unintentionally block the client from going any further than we ourselves have gone (Boden, 1988). Consequently, when the interactive process becomes more identifiable and understandable, countertransference becomes challenging, informative and helpful.

At the same time of recognizing our assets as disabled therapists, we also need to be able to recognize a number of common countertransferential pitfalls particularly in working with clients with disabilities. Any or all of these pitfalls may happen sequentially at any time during therapy or they may overlap concurrently.

Overidentification

In overidentification, we redefine the client's difficulty in terms of the disability and we may lose our clinical objectivity and/or minimize the client's problems. In the case of Marie, I overidentified with her when I could empathize with her pain of growing up as a lonely teenager, isolated and frustrated without knowing how to sign. Vacillating between the hearing and deaf world, she managed to sabotage attempts in therapy to develop healthier support systems. In my overidentification with her, I missed and minimized some cues of deeper pathology that signalled a borderline personality disorder with characteristic patterns of dysfunctional relationships, affective instability and recurrent self-destructive behaviors. Once I recognized the pattern, I changed my therapeutic style to address her disorder and put less emphasis on her hearing impairment.

Overestimation of Abilities

As female psychotherapists who are disabled, we have had to overcompensate to achieve what we have. We need to be aware of how our overachievement profile is an unusual one when we work with our clients with disabilities. Frequently, we may view clients with a disability as having more potential and being more capable than they really are. The danger lies in projecting onto the clients an overestimation of their ability to adjust and to "overcome" their disability.

Guilt and Anger

Guilt and anger, two sides of the same coin, are often related to overestimation of abilities. We may be angry at the client who doesn't get better or seem to benefit from positive identification with our disability. Likewise, the helpless client who lives as a victim may trigger unacceptable feelings of anger and frustration that counter what we have been taught in our own childhood, i.e., "helplessness/pity are useless." Further, we may begin to experience helplessness in our ability to help the client. Upon recognition of our anger, we may feel guilt if we confront the client and try to push them beyond their helplessness. As such, we may collusively allow the client to hide behind her disability.

Oversheltering

Because of our own experience, we understand the oppression of people who are disabled so therefore we may feel more protective of our clients than necessary–in fact, we may replicate the very form of oversheltering from which our clients may be trying to individuate. Another aspect of oversheltering that evokes counter-transferential feelings of helplessness and anger is a societal and/or familial one. This requires a systems point of view in order to make any effective changes. An example of this is when an adult client's helplessness is reinforced by parents who infantilize and sabotage their individuation. I am currently seeing a 24 year old woman who is deaf, whose first-generation Japanese parents are wealthy business owners. She works for the family business and gets paid a regular income regardless of her spotty work performance and difficulties with her co-workers. Further, they frequently bail her out of the local jail for various infractions including shoplifting, DWI's and drug deals. Whatever progress she makes in becoming independent, her parents unwittingly undo as their cultural mores dictate that they solve problems within the family rather than accepting professional help. Their enabling behavior is, thus, better understood as a cultural issue which requires a systems approach. Sadly and ironically, their efforts to help perpetuate the client's low self-esteem and pain.

Omnipotence and Overimportance

As a therapist with a disability, I often find myself in a double bind. I am aware of my reluctance to make referrals to or criticize non-disabled therapists who are not trained in working with people with disabilities. At the same time, I am highly protective of my clients who may suffer from the "ignorance" of well meaning therapists. The non-disabled therapists may be afraid to confront the client with a disability due to feeling guilty about their lack of knowledge about the disability. Consequently, non-disabled therapists may unwittingly collude with the client in their denial of the limitations of their disability. There is a risk, however, that the therapist who is disabled might assume an attitude of clinical superiority and perhaps place too much importance on our skills in working with disability issues. In essence, we may be carried away in wanting to become the "idealized disabled parent."

Co-Dependency

Across the board, we need to be aware of our sense of omnipotence and covert co-dependency in working with clients who are disabled, i.e., "Not only did I learn how to overcome barriers and take care of myself, I can also take care of you. Let me show you how . . ." We must remind ourselves to be part of their process and avoid our wish to show the client how to do "it." Appropriate assessment of how the disability fits into the total picture is instrumental, i.e., the client's ego strengths and weaknesses. Manifestations include giving too many suggestions, concrete answers and problem solving for clients without teaching them the process of doing it.

Resentment

Due to our uniqueness as women therapists who are disabled, we may find ourselves in demand. Tied in with our sense of omnipotence and codependency, we may be overly empathic and accept more low-fee referrals than may be realistically comfortable for us. As such, we may find ourselves resenting difficult or challenging clients. For example, I am the only licensed female therapist who knows sign language in an urban area covering a hundred mile radius. I frequently have difficulty in setting limits on accepting new low fee clients who are also disabled because they cannot find a therapist to work with them. Accordingly, I must continually evaluate my effectiveness as a therapist against my potential for burnout.

CONCLUSION

In this article, I have identified a number of common and unique transferential and countertransferential reactions and pitfalls that may be particularly relevant for therapists and clients who are disabled. The challenge of continually differentiating between the pathological and the situational and/or phenomenological is a constant one necessitating consistent monitoring and identification. Therapists who are disabled, by virtue of their uniqueness and constant clinical challenges, are encouraged to seek their own supervision to prevent burnout, ensure appropriate and optimal clinical practice in working with their clients who are disabled.

REFERENCES

Asch, A., & Rousso, H. (1985). Therapists with disabilities: Theoretical and clinical uses. *Psychiatry, 48,* 1-11.

Boden, R. (1988). Countertransference responses to lesbians with physical disabilities and chronic illnesses. In Shernoff, M. Scott, W. (Eds.) *Source book on lesbian and gay health care.*

De Wald, P. (1969). *Psychotherapy: A dynamic approach.* New York: Basic Books, Inc.

Eichenbaum, L., & Orbach, S. (1983). *Understanding women: A feminist psychoanalytic approach.* New York: Basic Books, Inc.

Gakis, T. (September 1990). Practitioner disability: What are the real handicaps? *Families in Society: The Journal of Contemporary Human Services.* Family Service Association.

Hall, G.C., & Malony, H.N. (1983). Cultural control in psychotherapy with minority clients. *Psychotherapy: Theory, Research and Practice, 20,* 131-142.

Malan, D. (1979). *Individual psychotherapy and the science of psychodynamics.* Boston: Butterworth, Inc.

Masterson, J. (1983). *Countertransference and psychotherapeutic technique.* New York: Bruner Mazel, Inc.

Rhodes, S. (1979). Communication and interaction in the worker-client dyad. *Social Service Review, 52* (1), 120-131.

Schwartz, M. (1978). Helping the worker with countertransference. *Social Work, 23,* 204-209.

Schwartz, R. (1989). When the therapist is gay: Personal and clinical reflections. *Journal of Gay and Lesbian Psychotherapy, 1*(1) 41-51.

Women and Physical Distinction:
A Review of the Literature
and Suggestions for Intervention

Sondra E. Solomon

SUMMARY. With few exceptions, the special concerns and status of women with physical distinctions (physical disability and facial disfigurement) have been largely ignored in the disability literature. Women with physical distinctions are perceived negatively and are devalued and marginalized in our culture. They face a double discrimination due to their gender and their disability. The situation is even more acute for ethnic minority women with physical distinctions. This paper will review the literature on women with physical distinctions and explore some of the issues for ethnic minority women with physical distinctions. Recommendations are offered for feminist therapists who work with this population.

INTRODUCTION

The literature on stigma, impairment and physical disadvantage has attempted to define what constitutes disability and to describe

Sondra E. Solomon, MA, is a doctoral candidate in clinical psychology at the University of Vermont. She is a Black American with a congenital disorder, neurofibromatosis (NF), and has been physically distinctive since birth. She is currently exploring the perceptions and experiences of ethnic minority women with facial distinctions.

Correspondence may be addressed to: Sondra E. Solomon, MA, Department of Psychology, University of Vermont, John Dewey Hall, Burlington, VT 05401.

[Haworth co-indexing entry note]: "Women and Physical Distinction: A Review of the Literature and Suggestions for Intervention." Solomon, Sondra E. Co-published simultaneously in *Women & Therapy* (The Haworth Press, Inc.) Vol. 14, No. 3/4, 1993, pp. 91-103; and: *Women with Disabilities: Found Voices* (ed: Mary E. Willmuth, and Lillian Holcomb) The Haworth Press, Inc., 1993, pp. 91-103. Multiple copies of this article/chapter may be purchased from The Haworth Document Delivery Center [1-800-3-HAWORTH; 9:00 a.m. - 5:00 p.m. (EST)].

the interactions of individuals who are able bodied and those who are disabled. Some definitions consider only individuals with physical, cognitive or behavioral impairments while other definitions include individuals with facial disfigurements. Whichever definition is used the literature is very clear in one regard, physically distinctive individuals occupy a separate role in our culture. It is also quite clear that the literature has failed to address the specific concerns of women with physical disabilities or facial disfigurements. "Despite the attention given to disability in general and certain impairments in particular, one category within the disabled population has received little recognition or study: women" (Deegan & Brooks, 1985, p.1). Furthermore, there is virtually no information on ethnic minority women with disabilities. This paper will explore the literature on women with disabilities and explore some of the concerns of ethnic minority women with disabilities. Several insights and recommendations for feminist intervention with this population are offered.

DEFINITIONS AND STATISTICS

Definitions

Where possible and appropriate when referring to what the literature has characterized as stigmatized, abnormal, aberrant, disfigured, or disabled individuals, the term *physically distinctive* will be used. This term is relatively benign and can be utilized and easily understood as a descriptor for this special group of women.

Most readers who are familiar with the disability literature have accepted the definitions presented by Scheer and Groce (1988). It is useful to repeat those definitions here as they are applicable to the current discussion:

> *IMPAIRMENT:* An abnormality or loss of any physiological or anatomical structure or function.
> *DISABILITY:* The consequences of an impairment. Any restriction or lack of ability to perform an activity in the manner or within the range considered appropriate for non-impaired individuals.

HANDICAP: The social disadvantage that results from an impairment or disability. (p. 24)

Impairment is biologically determined or can be acquired from a trauma or a disease process during some point in a person's life. Disability is the physical consequence of the impairment or how the impairment is manifested in the real world (e.g., a child is born with retinal atrophy which renders her visually impaired). Finally, handicap is the social consequence of an impairment or the expression of the impairment in a social context. Women with functional impairments are not intrinsically disabled or incapable of carrying out their personal, family, social and political responsibilities. It is the interaction of the physical limitations with social, environmental and cultural factors, and societal prejudice that determines whether or not a person is "disabled." Scheer and Groce (1988) believe that much of the strength of this conceptual framework lies in its emphasis on the importance of the social consequences of disability.

Statistics

It is difficult to determine how many women have a disabling condition or are physically distinctive. Obtaining sensitive, reliable data is difficult because there is no consensus regarding what constitutes a disabling condition. Furthermore, the numbers of physically distinctive women may be under-reported because women may be reluctant to label themselves as "disabled" or "impaired" and self report as members of a disenfranchised group. These labels are perceived as derogatory, belittling, and threatening to a woman's perceived status, self-worth, and role in society. Popular statistics regarding the prevalence of disability in the United States indicate that approximately 35 million Americans (1 in every 7) are affected by some disabling condition. What is troubling about this figure is that it is never clear which disabling conditions are included in the statistic. When the word "disability" is invoked, the common image is of an individual, most often male, in a wheelchair. Obviously, women, as well as men, have disabling conditions and there are various impairments that can be included under the rubric of "disability." These impairments may include physical impairments, (e.g., visual, auditory, motor), cosmetic distinctions (e.g., facial disfigurement), neurological disorders (e.g., multiple sclerosis), cognitive disorders (e.g., learning disabilities), and emotional disorders (e.g., schizophrenia, depression, anxiety, phobia). Asch and Fine (1988) write that "of the 51 percent of the nation that is female, we can estimate that one-sixth have disabilities" (Asch & Fine, 1988, p. 1). At a minimum, there may be 5.8 million women in the United States with disabilities.

Even if the discussion is limited to physical disability it is still difficult to describe the pattern of conditions that cause the impairments that render a woman physically distinctive. Physical impairment can be congenital or acquired from some disease process or traumatic injury. Pope and Tarlov (1991) report that "for young adults mobility limitations such as those caused by spinal cord injuries, orthopaedic impairments and paralysis are the most common causes. For middle aged and older adults, chronic diseases, especially heart, circulatory and vascular problems (e.g., stroke) or neurological disorders (e.g., multiple sclerosis) predominate as causes for limitation" (Pope & Tarlov, 1991, p. 2). Furthermore, advances in medicine and technology have achieved great success in averting the death of individuals who sustain injuries that render them impaired. For example, "in the 1950's only people with low level paraplegia were generally expected to survive. Today even people with high level quadriplegia are surviving" (Pope & Tarlov, 1991, p. 3).

The literature is less clear regarding what constitutes atypical facial types. Bull and Rumsey (1988) reviewed the literature on the social psychology of facial appearance and found that "the profound social significance of the face, taken together with society's prejudices toward those who have an atypical facial appearance can mean that an unattractive facial appearance could be a severe social handicap" (Bull & Rumsey, 1988, p.179). MacGregor (1981) adds that "the greatest concern is the large number of people with facial deviations who seem to be classified as marginal or forgotten people" (MacGregor, 1981, p. 28).

Some examples of facial distinction resulting from congenital factors include Apert's, Crouzon's and Teacher-Collins syndromes, lateral facial dysplasia (LFD), cranio-facial dysplasia (CFD), and neurofibromatosis (NF). Individuals can also acquire a facial distinction as a result of traumatic injury, disease process or burn.

WOMEN AND PHYSICAL DISTINCTION

The empirical data on women with physical distinctions (physical disability or facial disfigurement) are limited. Information regarding women with physical distinctions remains largely descriptive and anecdotal or comes from the writings of physically distinctive women themselves. Browne, Connors and Stern (1985), and Stewart (1989) are examples of such personal accounts. Although most studies include adult women and girls in their study samples, investigators still fail to address the special concerns of women with physical distinctions. The limited empirical data are infused with stereotyped attitudes about the physically distinctive woman's sexuality, post disability sexual function, and socially disadvantaged status. The perceptions and experiences of the women themselves are rarely offered. What is most often documented are the perceptions, attitudes and behaviors of able-bodied women and men when they interact with women with physical distinctions. DeHaan and Wallander (1988) report that the limited number of new studies of women and disability can be attributed to the fact that "of the newly disabled, approximately 78% are men" (DeHaan & Wallander, 1988, p. 145). Still, the research community has treated all women with disabilities in the aggregate, and has failed to acknowledge the differences between various types of disabilities (spinal cord injured v. blind v. amputee). Furthermore, researchers have only discussed the differences between disabled men and women in the most general terms. These studies have acknowledged that women with disabilities fare much worse than men with disabilities and non-disabled women but rarely discuss in detail the social forces promoting the differential treatment.

What is special about women with physical distinctions? There are a few investigators who have focused on the special concerns of women with distinctions (Asch & Fine, 1988; Deegan & Brooks, 1985; DeHaan & Wallander, 1988; Fallon, 1990; Frank, 1988). There is also wide consensus in the literature that all individuals with a physical impairment or atypical body or facial type belong to a population that is classified as marginal, forgotten, and socially disadvantaged (Bull & Rumsey, 1988; Davis, 1961; Friedson, 1965; Goffman, 1963; MacArthur, 1982; Myerson, 1988; Safilos-Roth-schild, 1970; Scott, 1969). The cultural demand to be pleasing in appearance is impossible to avoid and the demand is most emphatic for women. Fallon (1990) writes:

> Culturally bound and consensually validated definitions of what is desirable and attractive play an important part in the development of body image. One's body image includes her perception of the cultural standards, her perception of the extent to which she matches the standard, and the perception of the relative importance that members of the cultural group and the individual place on that match. (p. 81)

Researchers have acknowledged that women with physical distinctions are less likely to be employed, earn substantially less, fare much worse in times of economic crisis, and are less likely to be college educated than men with disabilities or non-disabled women (Greenblum, 1977; O'Toole & Weeks, 1978). Women with disabilities are also disadvantaged socially. Fine and Asch (1985) acknowledge that the woman with a physical distinction faces unusual social and economic realities and "while marriage may not be a preferred status for an increasing number of women, it is a customary measure of social options and position. Compared to non-disabled women, disabled women are more likely never to marry, marry at a later age and, once married, to be divorced" (p. 8).

   The negative attitudes, preconceptions and responses that perceived normal appearing others have towards all individuals with visible physical distinctions are wide ranging, have been endorsed in the literature and are part of our cultural legacy. Baker and Smith (1939) acknowledged that, "there are a number of patients with facial disfigurements, who have obtained very credible surgical results, yet have remained unsatisfied and have shown that they are sick and maladjusted persons" (p. 301). By 1948, the numbers of disabled individuals in the United States had risen dramatically as a result of combat injuries sustained by service women and men during World War II; however, little had changed regarding the way physically distinctive individuals were perceived. Myerson (1948) wrote that the locus of disability problems was viewed as being in the bodies of people characterized as disabled. It was thought that there was a destiny in disability and disfigurement and that "these people would lead deprived, marginal lives in a material and social world designed for the able-bodied" (p. 5). The solution to the problem, beyond what charity they could get from their families, doctors or social welfare agencies was to help them accept their fate by helping them to adjust to their environment. To attempt to alter hurtful, but traditional societal behavior was an unthinkable task. Goffman (1963) called "disability" an abomination of the body, a deformity and that by definition, the possessor of the stigma is not quite human. In fact, he titled his book *Stigma: Notes on the Management of a Spoiled Identity.*

In 1974, Berscheid and Walster published their work on the psychology of beauty. Their research influenced future inquiry in the psychology of appearance and purported that "a person's physical attractiveness is an extraordinary variable, for it accounts for a statistically significant variance in almost all social situations" (p. 161). The effect is that physically attractive individuals are preferred to less attractive individuals and receive numerous preferential social treatments. Berscheid and her colleagues did not consider physically distinctive individuals in her investigations. In the late 1970's and throughout the 1980's researchers focused on the importance of facial appearance and the disadvantaged status of the woman who possesses a facially distinctive appearance. By the 1990's, cultural attitudes have remained unchanged. Bernstein (1990) stated that:

> people with obvious deformities are disadvantaged in their social relations. People stare, and people make job determinations and reject persons with facial scars. The public reacts in terms of how upsetting a disfigured person is to them. Facially handicapped individuals are different in the roles they play in society than those of a person that is perceived as normal in appearance. Furthermore, if people are deformed, they may be converted into things, and treated in an altered manner. (p. 131)

Women with physical distinctions therefore face double discrimination. Able bodied women in our culture must conform to a narrowly defined standard of beauty which is quite different from the appearance standard that is imposed on men. There is a constant bias against unattractive women. The bias against women who are physically distinctive is even more profound. Women with distinctions (physical disability or facial disfigurement) are inevitably ostracized by society because of their gender and their impairment and are constantly challenged and frequently oppressed. "Disabled women are perceived as inadequate for economically productive roles (traditionally considered appropriate for males) and for the nurturant, reproductive roles considered appropriate for females" (Fine & Asch, 1985, p. 6). Our culture devalues women based on gender-linked stereotypes and assumptions and marginalizes or otherwise devalues all individuals with physical distinctions. Women with physical distinctions are always challenged because they possess these negatively valued characteristics.

ETHNIC MINORITY WOMEN
AND PHYSICAL DISTINCTION

What is the special case of ethnic minority women with physical distinctions? There are virtually no data on ethnic minority women with disabilities. This may stem, in part, from the fact that the research community as a whole has failed to address the concerns of ethnic minorities in all areas, not only disability. Ethnic minority women may be economically prohibited, due to inadequate health insurance or limited financial resources, from seeking medical and mental health services. Ethnic minority women may also be reluctant to seek mental health services because of the dearth of ethnic minorities in the mental and medical professions. They may perceive the ethnic minority therapist to be more sensitive to their needs and be reluctant to seek services from a White therapist.

What are the special concerns of the ethnic minority woman with a physical distinction? Claudette is a Black American woman with a pronounced craniofacial dysplasia due to a large tumor which has invaded the left side of her face. During an interview Claudette acknowledged that she has had a disparate social experience. She acknowledged that her social interactions were limited and quite different from her non-disabled Black and disabled White women friends, and most likely different from most every other person that she knew. She acknowledged that she had never known anyone in her family or in her limited circle of friends who looked like her and had few people with whom she could talk regarding the realities of her social experience. Claudette said that she kept her feelings to herself, which further exacerbated her feelings of isolation. Claudette also talked about her experience in public situations. She reported that she was never quite sure if people were giving her "the look" because she was Black or because she had a "different face." Claudette described "the look" as the double take, prolonged stare, or sneer she so often encountered on the street. She reported being denied seating near a window at a New York City restaurant, and that frequently people, Black and White, avoid sitting next to her on a crowded New York City bus or subway. At times it is impossible for her to attribute the discrimination she faces to her race or to her physical distinction. Claudette said that she believes her ethnicity and physical distinction weave a tapestry of negative attributes. At times she feels like a lightening rod, continually absorbing people's primitive fears, while she is forced to live separate and apart from the rest of society. Sometimes she says she feels alien, an observer of human interaction, rather than a participant in the human experience. Claudette's single voice may ring true for other women of color with physical distinctions, and be typical of other women in general with disabilities.

The ethnic minority woman is, in the first instance, doubly devalued because she is a woman and possesses a physical distinction. Also, as a member of an ethnic minority (e.g., African-American, Native American, Korean, Latina), the dominant culture further devalues her because of her ethnicity or race. Negative attributes do not exist in isolation. Women with multiple negative attributes are excessively challenged. For example, the woman who has a congenital disorder which renders her distinctive in appearance is vulnerable to many more negative reactions from others. She may suffer oppression because she is physically distinctive and at the same time face discrimination because of her race. She may be blind and have paraplegia and be Native American. It can be said that the ethnic minority woman or the woman with multiple disabilities is a survivor of a triple edged discrimination. It is impossible to report at this time how these women cope with their marginalized

status since no studies have reported their experience or perceptions. The literature has failed to address the experience of this
unique group.

FEMINIST INTERVENTIONS
WITH PHYSICALLY DISTINCTIVE WOMEN

What can the feminist therapist do to assist the woman or ethnic
minority woman with a physical distinction? What kind of help is
going to be most effective? Again, there is little research in this
area. It is never safe to presume that the woman is in the therapist's
office because of the physical distinction. It is important to recognize that the physical distinction and the individual are separate and
that the physical distinction may not be the most salient component
of the woman's self image. There may be a host of other precipi-
tants that compel her to seek assistance (e.g., incest, discrimination,
discomfort in initiating and maintaining social relationships, sexual
harassment). Allow the client to report in her own words the issues
that bring her to counseling at this point in time.

The feminist therapist can be most helpful in improving the
woman's self-esteem. While it is important to recognize that self-
esteem and physical distinction are critical issues, they should not
be viewed out of the context of other social factors (e.g., class, age,
education, ethnicity).

It is also not safe to presume that the client's silence about her
physical distinction means that it is not important or irrelevant. A
White American woman, with a facial birthmark, acknowledged
what she has described as a "conspiracy of silence" with a former
therapist. She described the silence as the failure to name the physical difference and process its meaning for both client and therapist.
She reported that the silence served to recapitulate her childhood
experience with her family, and stimulated the memory of various
painful episodes with friends and strangers throughout her life.
These issues were never discussed in session because the physical
distinction was never named.

Also, it is not safe, a priori, to presume that the client with a
physical distinction requires help, information and social support.
The woman may be extremely knowledgeable about her medical

status and have current information about her disability. Alternatively, the woman may be overwhelmed by a sense of isolation and loneliness. These feelings stem, in part, because she may have never known another person who looks like her and may have limited knowledge about her physical distinction. In this instance the feminist therapist would be most helpful in the role of facilitator, assisting the client in establishing a network or support group, and helping her to obtain information about her health status.

The feminist therapist may also be called upon as advocate. In workshops held with a colleague, Pat Fontaine, we were struck by the way both able-bodied and disabled therapists constructed a hierarchy of disabilities and doled out sympathy and support in direct proportion to the perceived severity of the disability. Some workshop participants were reluctant to consider some types of difference (e.g., facial disfigurement) as worthy of intervention. As feminist therapists we must be willing to examine our own biases and preconceptions about disability and work to change the misconceptions and biases harbored by others.

CONCLUSION

Society exerts a negative influence on physically distinctive individuals, particularly women and ethnic minority women. The culture accomplishes this by stringently defining what is beautiful and what is not an acceptable physical appearance, and excludes those individuals who do not conform to the standard. This article has discussed how a physical distinction is construed to be a powerful negative attribute. Bernstein (1990) writes:

> The psychology of difference still dominates our society and when the differences are not racial or cultural but are handicaps, they bring to the fore our own fears of fragility. Most people are therefore eager to segregate the maimed and unsightly, just as there is a resistance to close association among many racial groups. (p. 139)

As feminist therapists we must be aware of this cultural dynamic and of its negative influence on the lives of our physically distinctive clients.

REFERENCES

Asch, A., & Fine, M. (1988). Introduction: Beyond pedestals. In A. Asch & M. Fine (Eds.), *Women with disabilities* (pp. 1-37). Philadelphia, PA: Temple University Press

Baker, W.Y., & Smith, L.H. (1939). Facial disfigurement and personality. *Journal of the American Medical Association. 112;* 301-304.

Bernstein, N.R. (1990). Objective bodily damage: Disfigurement and dignity. In T.F. Cash, & T. Pruzinsky (Eds.), *Body images: Development, deviance and change.* N.Y.: Guilford Press

Berscheid, M.E., & Walster, E. (1974). Physical attractiveness. In L. Berkowitz (Ed.), *Advances in Experimental and Social Psychology.* Vol. 7. N.Y.: Random House.

Browne, S.E., Connors, D., & Stern, N. (1985). *With the power of each breath: A disabled women's anthology.* P.A.: Cleis Press.

Bull, R., & Rumsey, N. (1988). *The social psychology of facial appearance.* N.Y.: Springer-Verlag.

Davis, F. (1961). Deviance disavowal: The management of strained interaction to the visibly handicapped. *Social Problems. 9,* 120-132.

Deegan, M.J., & Brooks, N.A. (1985). Women and disability: The double handicap. In M.J. Deegan, & L.W. Brooks (Eds.), *Women and disability: The double handicap* (pp. 1-5). N.J.: Transaction Books.

DeHaan, C.B., & Wallander, J.L. (1988). Self-concept, sexual knowledge and attitudes, and parental support in the sexual adjustment of women with early- and late-onset physical disability. *Archives of Sexual Behavior. 17,* 145-161.

Fallon, A. (1990). Culture in the mirror: Sociocultural determinants of image. In T. F. Cash, & T. Pruzinsky (Eds.), *Body images: Development, deviance and change* (pp.80-109). New York: Guilford Press.

Fine, M., & Asch, A. (1985). Disabled women: Sexism without the pedestal. In M.J. Deegan, & Brooks, N.A. (Eds.), *Women and disability: The double handicap* (pp. 6-22). N.J.: Transaction Books.

Frank, G. (1988). Beyond stigma: Visibility and self-empowerment of persons with congenital limb deficiencies. *Journal of Social Issues. 44,* 95-116.

Friedson, E. (1965). Disability as social deviance. In M.B. Sussman (Ed.), *Sociology and rehabilitation.* Washington, D.C.: American Sociological Association.

Goffman, E. (1963). *Stigma: Notes on the management of a spoiled identity.* N.J.: Prentice Hall Press.

Greenblum, J. (1977). Effect of vocational rehabilitation on employment and earnings of the disabled: State variations. *Social Security Bulletin 40* (12), 3-166.

MacArthur, L. (1982). Judging a book by its cover: A cognitive analysis of the relationship between physical appearance and stereotyping. In A. Hastorff and A. Isen (Eds.), *Cognitive social psychology.* N.Y.: Elsevier Press.

MacGregor, F. (1981). Patient dissatisfaction with results of technically satisfactory surgery. *Aesthetic Plastic Surgery. 5,* 27-32.

Myerson, L. (1948). Physical disability as a social psychological problem. *Journal of Social Issues. 4* (4), 2-10.

Myerson, L. (1988). The social psychology of physical disability. *Journal of Social Issues. 44* (1), 175-188.

O'Toole, J., & Weeks, C. (1978). *"What happens after school" A study of disabled women and education.* San Francisco: Women's Educational Equity Communications Network.

Pope, A.M., & Tarlov, A.R. (1991). *Disability in America: Towards a national agenda for prevention.* National Academy Press: Washington, D.C.

Safilos-Rothschild, C. (1970). *The sociology and social psychology of disability and rehabilitation.* N.Y.: Random House.

Scheer, J., & Groce, N. (1988). Impairment as a human constant: Cross-cultural and historical perspectives on variation. *Journal of Social Issues. 44* (1), 23-37.

Scott, R. (1969). *The making of blind men.* N.Y.: Russell Sage.

Stewart, J. (1989). *The body's memory.* N.Y.: St. Martin's Press.

An Account of the Search of a Woman Who Is Verbally Impaired for Augmentative Devices to End Her Silence

Lisa Fay

SUMMARY. This article reveals through personal narrative that speech production may not be the optimum goal for women with communication impairments. Emphasizing speech production may be detrimental to women's mental health, considering that communication impairments are the least amenable to medical treatments (Baker, 1983; Baker, Stump, Nyberg & Conti, 1991). Speech therapists contend that with enough therapy I won't need a device. While speech therapy has its place, exhausting therapy does not enhance life (Sacks, 1989). After many years of therapy I have plateaued without meeting speech standards and still face stigmatization from society (Van Riper, 1972). Therefore, it has become clear that I need technological intervention to improve the communicative quality of my life (Hahn, 1991). Extending augmentative communication devices to other verbally-impaired women will mean discovering new ways to solve old problems, i.e., giving women more choices in determining whether to use technology for their communication difficulties (Scherer & McKee, 1990). This self-determination is in contrast to

---

Lisa Fay is a poet, activist, and artist who wants to tell people about better ways of living.

Correspondence may be addressed to: Lisa Fay, One Peterborough Street, Apt. 10, Boston, MA 02215-4406.

[Haworth co-indexing entry note]: "An Account of the Search of a Woman Who Is Verbally Impaired for Augmentative Devices to End Her Silence." Fay, Lisa. Co-published simultaneously in *Women & Therapy* (The Haworth Press, Inc.) Vol. 14, No. 3/4, 1993, pp. 105-115; and: *Women with Disabilities: Found Voices* (ed: Mary E. Willmuth, and Lillian Holcomb) The Haworth Press, Inc., 1993, pp. 105-115. Multiple copies of this article/chapter may be purchased from The Haworth Document Delivery Center [1-800-3-HAWORTH; 9:00 a.m. - 5:00 p.m. (EST)].

105

the medical profession making choices for them (American Speech and Hearing Association, 1991).

I never thought I would be writing these words. I know it is best for me to use a voice synthesizer. It might be unusual for people to see me with a synthesizer, a technical means to communicate. However, more of me and what I want to say will come out with a synthesizer. Having a voice synthesizer doesn't mean I won't talk at all, it just means I will be able to use what I have more effectively. When I am communicably-impaired, I will use the synthesizer. This is my story of being the most verbal woman to request a synthesizer (H. Shane, personal communication 1990, 1991; B. Romich, personal communication, December, 1990).

A revolution in my own thinking took place over 20 years. From childhood, I was taught to speak regardless of the effort it entailed or how I was feeling about treatment. An incident occurring in November 1990 was the straw that broke the camel's back. I called a Boston publisher to encourage him to publish a poetry anthology. When I got him on the phone, he said, "Speak, speak." The way he said it stuck in my brain. I could not speak automatically when I wanted to speak.

I can no longer go along with what the medical community wants of me, and that is more therapy. My speech therapists think that if I have more therapy then I won't need a device. But having more therapy is futile as I will explain in this paper.

Women are often afraid to say no. They equate quitting with losing. I found peace by quitting. What makes this situation difficult is that at times I have extraordinarily articulate speech. I am most verbal on higher speech functions, such as conversing intelligibly on many topics. I falter on personal information data such as names, numbers, and addresses, which are lower on the hierarchy of speech functions. I am highly verbal on a narrow test band. However, my communication peters out rather quickly. Sometimes, I get tired and run out of air. It takes an extraordinary amount of energy to talk, requiring involvement of undeveloped speech and jaw muscles.

This story begins on Dec. 1, 1955 when I was born 10 weeks early. In the beginning, my mother noticed I didn't hear well when she read bedtime stories. The other children would lie down and I would sit up. My mother took me to the doctor at age 2 1/2 and he found nothing. At age 4 1/2, when I wasn't talking and walking, she took me to the doctors and they diagnosed cerebral palsy. Cerebral palsy is brain damage which can affect all daily functions of living, such as speaking, eating, walking, dressing, seeing, thinking, breathing, and hearing. Most persons with cerebral palsy have speech and motor problems. This paper will concentrate on the communication portion.

I have had the most treatment for stuttering so I will give it the most attention. I don't remember just what incident prompted stuttering but I do recall my mother taking me to speech therapy at age six for articulation problems. Prolonging the vowels was emphasized at that time and still is the method most used. Stuttering therapy began for me when I was eight or nine years old. My childhood was severely limited by defective speech. Other kids laughed at me, mimicked my stutter, or refused to let me play with them–and adults were no better.

My mouth felt like an animal trap most of the time. The more I tried to open it, the more it slammed shut. There were times when I didn't talk for weeks, and my family said they didn't know me. How could I tell them with such a trap for a mouth? It is hard for any family to understand the problem, but I was never shunned.

Teachers either ignored me or were hell-bent on having me speak. Once, in the sixth grade, I gave a speech on a flower, either the goldenrod or the magnolia. I stuttered on every word, much to the teacher's horror. The kids may have laughed at me, but I knew what counted most, having always made the honor roll.

The worst part about being a stutterer is that I never know when I am going to stutter. I may be talking well, and then block in the beginning, the middle, or the end of the word; sometimes it is all three.

Sometimes I cannot understand words or cannot say them so I block, due to undeveloped speech muscles. My jaw bone is also undeveloped. Often the words and the sounds which are hard for the child to produce are the same ones with which the stutterer struggles. I hate it terribly when I stutter on the most personal description, my name; and it is such a short one.

After I stutter, I feel like a ruptured sewage tank, leaking anger. What I really need is a hug. This unpredictability is nerve-wracking and delays my personal adjustment and social growth in this fast-paced world. I was told at the Mind/Body Institute at New England Deaconess Hospital (1992) and Goode, Schrof, and Burke (1991) have reported that those with facial tension have more unhappy thoughts and feelings.

Van Riper (1972) said the speech of persons with cerebral palsy resembles stuttering behavior: "Often the extreme tension that characterizes spasticity will produce articulatory contacts so hard as to resemble or engender stuttering symptoms" (p. 380).

Stuttering is not disfiguring nor does it mean a loss of body part. The anatomy of communication is usually intact. What it does involve is dysfluency of timing. Some experts may disagree with my definition, but they have no problem identifying the disorder when they see it. Stutterers are known for prolonging words or blends, eye-blinking, twitching, licking the tongue, blocking and facial contortions. Unfortunately, I do all of the above.

During my college years in the 1970s, I tried to tell my vocational rehabilitation counselor just how stuttering affected my life. Keeping friends was difficult and my education suffered immeasurably as I rarely spoke. I told him that, without help, my potential as a writer would be forever limited as communication skills via speaking are absolutely essential.

He ignored my pleas, saying it wasn't a real problem since I never stuttered badly with him. This was partially correct since I had grown accustomed to him. But he never saw me in new social situations, schools, parties and family gatherings, where I never failed to bomb. Nothing is so central to personality development as communication. Very little of life exists without it.

There were several events which led me to believe I had a problem. I was a sports editor for the Framingham State College newspaper, responsible for assigning and writing articles. I could not speak under pressure, and my head boiled with turmoil. I vowed never to torture myself this way again. I loved the work I was doing, but there had to be a better way of doing it, I told myself.

While still enrolled at Framingham, I spent a semester abroad in London. After my British studies, I went to Zurich and stopped in a youth hostel run by nuns. I was tired and stuttered very badly, and had terrible word-finding problems. The nun dialed a number and said, "Come with me." I had no speech to say, "Where are you taking me?" She put me in a cab and the cabbie drove me to a drug addiction clinic in Zurich. The counselors laughed and sent me back to the hostel five hours later.

When it came time for work after I graduated from college in 1978, the same problems intensified. I had no problem getting interviews as I had a good resumé. But, on all of my fifty interviews, I stuttered terribly.

The 1990 Massachusetts Rehabilitation Commission Study on Women and Disability found that the vocational rehabilitation system was not addressing the issue of women with speech problems (Massachusetts Rehabilitation Commission, 1990). Speech therapy alone does not make women employable. Anecdotal accounts contained comments such as these:

> The counselors have tried very hard to come up with ideas for me, but there's a basic notion that my speech is too much of an impediment, and that I can't work with people. (p. 7)

> More jobs for people with speech problems, maybe with computers or video. (p. 13)

Not only are the needs of women with speech problems not being addressed by the vocational rehabilitation system, but women face gender bias in gaining VR services (Menz et al., 1989; Russo & Jansen, 1988) and have a hard time obtaining gadgets that would make them employable (Vash, 1982). Scherer and McKee (1990) reported that women tend to have less exposure to technical innovations and therefore are uninformed and uninterested in what technology can do for them.

After a number of additional false starts, I was referred to Emerson College's Speech and Hearing Clinic which I attended from 1977 to 1981. During that time I made slow progress and was terminated for that reason. Experts generally concur that therapy must be intense and continuous to be successful. Since then I have tried two other programs. The programs exhausted me. The longer the day, the less fluent I became.

In December 1990, 20/20 had a TV show on stuttering and Barbara Walters said that they received more letters on stuttering than on any other issue. They get more requests to repeat that show than any other.

Even my psychotherapist did not understand stuttering (Fay, 1982). He seemed to think I could stop stuttering instantly like turning off a T.V. set. He liked to say, "You do it to yourself, Lisa."

My final effort came from Massachusetts General Hospital where treatment emphasized wordfinding problems. Because stuttering was so obvious, it was hard to diagnose wordfinding problems. I usually gesture with my hands, saying, "Do you know what I mean?" Sometimes, I use sign language, what little I know. I was discharged again in 1987, having reached a plateau in terms of development.

While therapists concentrated on stuttering, they ignored the fact that I can be nonverbal at times. I noticed this happening when I ran for several years. It had always been that way, but I noticed it when a runner said, "You never talk when you run." He did me a favor, I stopped running. I'd rather talk than run races. Besides, I already had all the letters, ribbons, and trophies I wanted.

There was also a time when I had a date and I did not say one word, from the time I got in the car to the time he took me home. My eyes became the only expressor of feelings. Of course, you don't necessarily have to speak on a date. However, I now cancel dates when I have no communicative abilities.

Even everyday situations can be vexing. One day, I was at the post office and just looked at the postman. He said, "Write down everything and come back."

Baclofen was tried to relax my muscles. Although the drug does have a soothing effect, it is not enough to overcome the overwhelming neurological deficits.

My speech does not stretch like cheese. As I get older, my speech is getting harder to understand as has been reported for others (Bodine & Beukelman, 1991). There is only so much you can rehabilitate any impaired asset. Then it breaks down . . . . totally.

The medical profession focuses on the substantial and multiple communication deficits, instead of on improving the quality of life. Somehow, they feel I can magically hop over these lifelong deficits by repetitive and constant rehabilitation and my life will be more normal.

Brandeis researcher Irving Zola (1991) used his airport travel as an example. When he began air travel over 30 years ago, he said his physical difficulties were minor even when vigorously probed. Twenty years later with the women's and the independent living movements in full swing and his physical condition relatively unchanged, his reactions were quite different:

> No longer was it necessary to prove that I was just like anyone else, if no better, "a supercrip." Though I was still capable of walking long distances, I no longer felt it was *necessary* to do so. And so, upon arrival at an airport after parking the car or being left off, I would get into either my own wheelchair or the airline's and into that distant terminal. Completely unanticipated was the difference in my physical condition at the end of my trip: I now arrived *un*tired and not needing of nap, not sore from sweating legs and tight braces, not cramped from the general strain of extra walking.
>
> .... only then did I realize how much of my travel "experience" inhered not in my disability but rather in the society in which I lived–socially maintained and socially constructed. (p. 4)

If therapy hasn't yet enabled me to communicate up to a standard, it never will. Of all medical problems, communication impairments are the most unamenable to treatment (Baker, 1983, Baker et al., 1991).

Campling (1981) writes of a woman, Diana, who is erroneously taught to get out speech no matter what it takes, often past her capacity. This woman is stressed out when trying to communicate, as well as frustrated over what is never said. Practitioners forget that too much therapy leaves no room for life (Sacks, 1989).

People must not look at me from a medical view anymore, but at what technology is best for my quality of life (Hahn, 1991; Scherer & McKee, 1990). They may not like it, but there is always room for revolutionary thought. Therapy has played its role, now it is time for technology to step in and take its place. After therapy, the question must be what is the next best way to release frustration. Hoffman (1986) said frustration is the key to granting speech technology. Shane (1985) acknowledged the need for technological intervention which "prevents development of other maladaptive behaviors and fosters the individual's capability to benefit from speech therapy" (p. 272).

It was against this historic backdrop that I entered Howard Shane's Communication Enhancement Center. His staff basically said that there wasn't anything out there for me, that I should use a tape recorder, and rehearse my speeches. It was then I decided to become Howard's "popesa." A popesa is an advisor to an authority. If I could change my attitudes, opinions, feelings about speech production, so can experts. It is important that they act on my suggestions, and not the other way around.

I went to "Project Tech" run by the Easter Seals Society. Their recommendations were better. They urged that another person tape my presentations and lectures. In addition, they recommended a Zygo Parrot. A Parrot is a small, hand-held digital recorder/play-back unit with space for 16 brief messages such as name, number, address, and so forth.

Somehow, these practitioners missed the point that I need a sense of balance in my life. It is nearly impossible to do all the rehabilitation required of me. I swim, and have regular massage and chiropractic treatments. Since it is harder to rehabilitate brain functions, such as speaking and thinking (Sienkiewicz-Mercer, 1989), I have chosen not to do more speech therapy. Whenever practitioners mention therapy, I think, "I'd rather be vacationing in Bali." Never do I hear any one of them say "relaxation."

Also, therapy was wearing down the jaw bones used to make speech, thereby making it harder for me to open my mouth. Too much therapy can actually make speech function deteriorate faster.

It is ironic that twenty-six people in my neighborhood signed letters in 1991 supporting my need for a device. Twenty-six community approvals speak more loudly than three negative medical reports. Sometimes, the community knows better than the medical profession. The community knows a synthesizer will help me do justice to my intelligence and my large Boston social circle.

The American Speech and Hearing Association (ASHA) makes a grave error in stating that only those who are nonspeaking are eligible for devices (ASHA, 1991). Did these professionals ever think to ask their clients who are speech-impaired whether *they* wanted devices? The ones who have the problem should determine if they want devices, not the medical community (Scherer & McKee, 1990). Women who are speech-impaired for whatever reason do not communicate to the fullest extent possible.

To be eligible for devices, it is not enough to show gestural, written, and spoken impairments alone. Since I am unable to meet the speech standards in this society, I should be eligible to receive augmentative devices appropriate to my needs. Even though present technology cannot meet all the needs of speech-impaired women to share complex needs and feelings, their needs should at least be recognized in the ASHA statement. It is frustrating for these women not to be able to say all they think and feel, just as it is for nonverbal women not to speak at all.

To date, I use a Telecommunication Device for the Deaf (TDD) to supplement my communication. Although Project Tech recommended a Zygo Parrot, as yet, it has not arrived. Elmer Bartels of the Massachusetts Rehabilitation Commission thought about my using a TDD until something better comes along. Using the TDD has proven to be a boon to my mental health. Details such as reservations, appointments, conversations with public officials, times, library information, and so forth are handled through the TDD. My body does not jump and jerk, my face does not struggle and strain. My body relaxes while I type like Mozart. My mental health does not feel so mutilated anymore.

It is evident from this paper that much needs to be done regarding women and speech impairments. Therapists must identify such women clients and refer them to an assistive technology center in their state. They must also encourage their clients to use technology to supplement their communication once their therapies have plateaued. Fine and Asch (1988) say it best:

> We need more information about women whose disabilities may be less immediately noticeable, but are of no less concern to their emotional, social, or economic lives. Or because they have said less, can one conclude that such disabilities are less of an issue and that these women have less to tell? (p. 333)

I have said less in my life not because I wanted to, but because I couldn't say all I wanted to say. Hopefully, that won't be for much longer.

AUTHOR NOTE

Lisa Fay would like to thank the following people who contributed to the making of this paper: The Access Center at the Boston Public Library which provided me with extensive use and training on their computer equipment on which this article was typed and printed. Elmer Bartels, Massachusetts Rehabilitation Commission, who recommended the TDD and to June Holt of the MRC Library who helped me with advice and articles. Mary Kay Cordill of Boston who helped give this paper a feminist perspective. Barbara Neumann of Roxbury, Massachusetts who provided hands-on editing to give this paper proper recognition, and Gloria Steinem (1983) who taught me that people who have the problem are the experts and not the experts themselves, and for writing that famous line, "Serious opposition is a measure of success" (p. 380) which helped keep me sane.

REFERENCES

American Speech and Hearing Association (1991). Committee on augmentative and alternative communication, Position statement. *American Speech and Hearing Association*, Supplement No. 5, *33*, 8-12.

Baker, B. (1983). Communication disabilities–An overview. *Rehabilitation/ WORLD*, *7*, 3-7.

Baker, B., Stump, R. T., Nyberg, E. H., & Conti, R. V. (1991). Augmentative communication and vocational rehabilitation. *Vocational Rehabilitation*, *1*, 72-83.

Bodine, C., & Beukelman, D. R. (1991). Predictions of future speech performance among potential users of AAC systems: A survey. *Augmentative and Alternative Communication*, *7*, 100-111.

Campling, J. (Ed.). (1981). *Images of ourselves: Women with disabilities talking.* Boston: Routledge & Kegan Paul.

Fay, L. (1982). An account of the psychotherapeutic process from the perspective of a client with a disability. *Women & Therapy*, *1*, 111-115.

Fine, M., & Asch, A. (1988). Epilogue: Research and politics to come. In M. Fine & Asch, A. (Eds.), *Women with disabilities: Essays in psychology, culture, and politics* (pp. 333-335). Philadelphia: Temple University Press.

Goode, E. E., Schrof, J., & Burke, S. (1991, June 24). Where emotions come from. *US News & World Report*, pp. 54-62.

Hahn, H. (1991). Alternative views of empowerment: social services and civil rights. *Journal of Rehabilitation*, *57*, 17-19.

Hoffman, A. C. (1986). There is funding out there. *Communication Outlook*, *7*, 8.

Massachusetts Rehabilitation Commission (1990). A Joint Study by The Project on Women and Disability & Massachusetts Rehabilitation Commission. Survey of women clients of the Massachusetts Rehabilitation Commission, pp. 1-20. Copies may be obtained by writing to: MRC Library, Mass. Rehab. Commission, Fort Point Place, 27-43 Wormwood Street, Boston, MA 02210-1606.

Menz, F. E., Hansen, G., Smith, H., Brown, C., Ford, M., & McCrowey, G. (1989). Gender equity in access, services and benefits from vocational rehabilitation. *Journal of Rehabilitation, 55*, 31-40.

Russo, N. F., & Jansen, M. A. (1988). Women, work, and disability: opportunities and challenges. In M. Fine & A. Asch (Eds.), *Women with disabilities: Essays in psychology, culture, and politics* (pp. 229-244). Philadelphia: Temple University Press.

Sacks, O. (1989). *Seeing voices.* Berkeley: University of California Press.

Scherer, M., & McKee, B. (1990). The assistive technology device predisposition assessment. *Communication Outlook, 12*, 23-27.

Shane, H. (1985). Selection of augmentative communication systems. In E. Cherow (Ed.), *Hearing-impaired children and adults with developmental disabilities* (pp.270-292). Washington DC: Gallaudet College Press.

Sienkiewicz-Mercer, R. (1989). *I raise my eyes to say yes.* Boston: Houghton-Mifflin.

Steinem, G. (1983). *Outrageous acts and everyday rebellions.* New York: Holt, Rinehart, and Winston.

Van Riper, C. (1972). *Speech correction: principles and methods* (5th ed.). Englewood Cliffs: Prentice Hall, Inc.

Vash, C. L. (1982). Employment issues of women with disabilities. *Rehabilitation Literature, 43*, 197-208.

Zola, I. K. (1991). Bringing our bodies and ourselves back in: Reflections on a past, present, and future "medical sociology." *Journal of Health and Social Behavior, 32*, 1-16.

What We Know About Women's Technology Use, Avoidance, and Abandonment

Marcia J. Scherer

SUMMARY. With the increasing availability of assistive technologies, persons with disabilities have unprecedented opportunities for full societal participation. But women, especially women with disabilities, have typically not had much exposure to and experience with technologies and can find them intimidating and frustrating. While many women use technologies regularly and with satisfaction, others use them infrequently and with reluctance, avoid them entirely, or try them only to abandon their use. This article discusses factors associated with technology use, avoidance, or abandonment as being outcomes of the interaction of: (a) The particular technology (design, service delivery), (b) the person's abilities and personality (judgment, expectations), (c) characteristics of the disability (type, severity), and (d) the person's psychosocial environment (social support, training and education). Assessment instruments exist to comprehensively profile individuals in the four areas so the most appropriate technologies can be recommended and needed modifications to technologies made.

Marcia Scherer has been doing research on technology use and non-use since 1985. Her primary objective is to have technologies viewed as *one* way of enhancing quality of life.

Correspondence may be addressed to: Marcia J. Scherer, PhD, National Technical Institute for the Deaf and International Center for Hearing and Speech Research, Rochester Institute of Technology, 1 Lomb Memorial Drive, Rochester, NY 14623.

[Haworth co-indexing entry note]: "What We Know About Women's Technology Use, Avoidance, and Abandonment." Scherer, Marcia J. Co-published simultaneously in *Women & Therapy* (The Haworth Press, Inc.) Vol. 14, No. 3/4, 1993, pp. 117-132; and: *Women with Disabilities: Found Voices* (ed: Mary E. Willmuth, and Lillian Holcomb) The Haworth Press, Inc., 1993, pp. 117-132. Multiple copies of this article/chapter may be purchased from The Haworth Document Delivery Center [1-800-3-HA-WORTH; 9:00 a.m. - 5:00 p.m. (EST)].

117

Transportation, education, health care, employment, even household management, have all become highly "technicalized." Additionally, women with disabilities have available many personal or assistive technologies to enhance their functioning. While many women use assistive technologies regularly and with great satisfaction, many others use them infrequently and with reluctance, avoid them entirely, or try them only to abandon their use. Women are significantly overrepresented in the last three categories primarily because they were not socialized and educated to become technically competent.

Assistive technologies or devices are mechanical, electrical, or computerized tools for enhancing the routine functioning of people who have physical limitations (disabilities). When people speak of "high-tech assistive devices" or "assistive technologies," they are usually referring to ones with electronic components. Computers per se are not considered assistive technologies. Rather, they are an access technology which means many devices operate and work through the control of a computer.

There are several ways to categorize assistive technologies: One is the degree of customization required (from a uniquely fabricated device to modifications in ones used by the general population). Another is according to functional purpose for which the device or assistive technology is prescribed. Three examples are:

1. Mobility devices: powered wheelchair systems, vehicle control systems, and sonic guides.
2. Augmentative and alternative communication (AAC) systems: technologies that enable a person with limited speech or no useable speech to visually display their communication or speak through synthesized speech output.
3. Sensory devices: reading devices for people with visual impairments; personal FM systems for persons with hearing loss.

It remains a fact that learning, workplace, and assistive technologies offer the best chance for persons with disabilities (male or female) to participate in today's mainstream society. Unfortunately, however, there is a tendency to see assistive technologies as being primary solutions to the typically complex process of rehabilitation.

It is common to hear optimistic statements about a person's quality of life being high once "she is enabled to walk (or talk, see, hear)" and "once the assistive device arrives." A state of affairs currently exists in which we often find ourselves considering widespread environmental accommodations and more and better devices for individuals, and not the provision of more intangible and indefinable psychosocial opportunities. The economic costs of such "individual deficit modification" may be high, but the emotional investment is low. Yet, to those who look to technology to enhance a person's quality of life and not merely to restore capability, it is ultimately more important and cost effective to consider the functions of devices and physical modifications within a comprehensive context of varying user interests, needs, and capabilities.

THE NEED FOR A MODEL WHEN MATCHING A PERSON AND A TECHNOLOGY (MPT)

We know that the highest rate of assistive technology use occurs (a) the more limited an individual's functioning and (b) when viable alternatives to use do not exist or are not available. For example, a woman born with cerebral palsy who has little or no intelligible speech will be a more frequent user of a computerized communication system than one who has difficulty with only certain words.

Ultimately, the goal of rehabilitation professionals is to find methods for matching a particular device with an individual in a way that will increase the likelihood of successful use and enhance the person's quality of life. Regardless of the type of device under consideration, an individual will either be a user or non-user of it. But people can vary within the categories of use/non-use: Use can be full-time and done willingly, or partial and done reluctantly (this most frequently occurs with persons whose device use is not optional or where a person will use a device in one environment but not another); non-use can be due to the avoidance of a device altogether (e.g., a person will not show up for an evaluation/fitting or will not purchase it) or to its abandonment.

One method of organizing the myriad influences on the use or non-use of a particular technology by a person is according to:

1. The characteristics of the *M*ilieu (environment and psychosocial setting) in which the assistive technology is used,
2. Pertinent features of the individual's *P*ersonality and temperament, and
3. The salient characteristics of the assistive *T*echnology itself.

This organization has been used to develop a "Matching Person and Technology (MPT)" model. Appendix A organizes the characteristics of persons who optimally use devices or who use them partially/reluctantly as compared to those who abandon the use of them or who avoid their use altogether according to each MPT category.

The MPT model can provide a broad as well as in-depth profile of where certain persons may be at a particular point in time with their devices. For example, a person may look like a partial/reluctant device user as far as the *Milieu*, but appear to be an optimal user according to the characteristics listed for *Personality* and *Technology*. Thus, the *Milieu* of use may need some intervention or modification for the person to gain maximum satisfaction and functional gain from use of the device.

Assistive device use is interactive among the above categories. That is, an alteration in one will have an affect on the others. For example, optimal use of one assistive device may likely lead to enthusiasm for trying another device, an improved self-esteem, and a wider social milieu. It is also the case that a person can be in one category with one device at a particular point in time and be in another with a second device at the same point in time. Further, the introduction of a new device can make the use of an existing one more complicated or cumbersome. It is likely that as time goes on, device compatibility/incompatibility will be a growing area of concern since we've become aware that a "fatal threshold" can be reached where a system composed of one or more devices has an additive effect of resulting in a situation of frustration and "overload" for a person and even such difficulties as "repetitive motion injuries."

CHARACTERISTICS OF THE MILIEU

Consumers of assistive technology services include persons with disabilities (primary consumers) and their family members and caretakers (secondary consumers). It is important to involve at the outset all who will be affected by the assistive technology, keeping in mind the function to which the technology will be put and the environment in which it will operate and be used.

One of the most common reasons for the non-use or reluctant use of an assistive technology is that it was forced upon the person by family members or therapists. Just as some families will resist the use of technological assistance, as many will purchase anything they believe will help only to discover that the individual either does not want to use it or cannot use it. Women, regardless of age, seem especially prone to such external direction.

Exposure and Opportunity. Factors such as environmental accommodations, available resources (e.g., private insurance for specialized treatment) and special opportunities (e.g., placement in a rehabilitation center with the newest equipment) are also important *Milieu* characteristics.

Socialization and education, particularly for those with congenital disabilities, play an important role, as one woman describes:

> Many people with congenital disabilities always had someone to take care of them. They never had to cope with things and they haven't developed those skills, they never learned them. Also, they tend to have low opinions of their abilities–'I can't feed myself,' 'I can't do the simplest things other people take for granted.' To be a successful user of a device requires patience and perseverance. Suffocating families and institutions sap individuals of that, of enthusiasm, the hope that something new and exciting can still happen. When you see an assistive device as an opportunity to better your life and situation, then you're willing to pay the price of a long, tiring, frustrating trial-and-error period of learning. If the desire and perseverance aren't there, the frustration is too great and after a short trial the device is shoved in the closet because it was too much of a hassle or it was just too overwhelming.

Women have traditionally grown up in dependent roles, with few technology-using role models, and encouraged to be docile and uncomplaining. While research shows that this is true for women in general (e.g., American Association of University Women, 1992; Gilligan, 1982), it is especially the case for women with disabilities.

Expectations. The attitudes of others and their expectations of the person, as expressed through intimate interactions or through exposure to the values of society as a whole, can have a profound influence on individuals and their expectations of themselves. A person's self-concept, motivation and aspirations are all shaped by social interactions and support that serve to control positive personal regard, resources and opportunities.

Social Support. An acquired disability often places sudden strains on family relationships and social resources. When the support network is altered, the person may experience both psychological and physical distress, which can lead to a further disorganization, deterioration, and disintegration of the social support system.

While not all social ties are supportive–and when effective supportive aid is given it is important to know under what conditions the aid was actually given (i.e., what was said or done to attract that positive aid)–assistive device users tended to have more social support than non-users. For example, their families built ramps and modified the family home or their employer held a job for them. Family reluctance to have the person return home unaided, stable family relations, and having a key family role, were all positively associated with assistive technology use.

The individual's cultural identity and the values and norms of that culture should be considered. For example, persons who wear hearing aids are viewed as rejecting Deaf Culture. There may also be cultural (and/or age) barriers to help-seeking in general.

CHARACTERISTICS OF THE PERSON

Technical Comfort. The assumption that all people with disabilities have the desire to effectively utilize a computer operated device is not an accurate one. Women in our society have traditionally received little exposure to technical perspectives and tend to be uninformed about computers and disinterested in the complex and sophisticated products of rehabilitation engineering efforts (Littrell, 1991).

For women who appear to be uncomfortable with or intimidated by technologies, the potential of achieving limited gains through the use of an assistive device is not worth the anxiety or discomfort involved in its use. As noted in the following quote from a woman rehabilitation professional, this situation will no doubt change as women become increasingly exposed to technologies at very young ages:

> I think younger people coming along will do much better. Most children with disabilities today are exposed to computers at a fairly young age. So a computer to them is not a strange box that they don't know how to operate. It's no more strange than their wheelchair or eyeglasses. For those seeing their first computer at the age of fifty, and who managed for fifty years without it, the device doesn't make a big enough difference to warrant all that effort to learn to use it. This is a transition time. In thirty years everyone will have equipment.

Women without the education, socialization or exposure to the use of a computer can have a distrust of it and exhibit anxiety when faced with one. Being anxious makes it more difficult to learn the skills to operate it. When feeling anxious about the use of a technology in public, interactions with others can become more strained, especially since assistive devices serve as signs of disability and set a person apart as being different. They can both physically and socially separate persons with disabilities from those without disabilities. Since a person's self-esteem and self-image are built up over time through interactions with other persons, assistive devices serve as symbols which have the ability to define those interactions and ultimately a person's self-image. For women who have been taught to emulate physical beauty, softness, and social grace, mechanical devices can be particularly "handicapping."

Cognitive Abilities and Aptitude. People differ in their aptitudes to effectively use assistive devices. The more sophisticated any device is, the more complicated the training may be in how to use that device.

The emphasis technology places on cognitive and intellectual capabilities, as opposed to motor and physical skills, has opened many opportunities for persons with physical disabilities but has created some barriers for women who were not allowed to pursue courses in math and science. Yet, learning styles typifying women can place them at an advantage: Women tend to have a *divergent* approach to problem-solving (seeing many solutions or possibilities) as opposed to a *convergent* approach which attempts to focus on the one best solution. When learning new information, they may also modify or expand their existing knowledge base and *accommodate* new ideas more easily than men who have been trained to try and fit new information into an existing schema (*assimilation*). Thus, while women may have some disadvantages as far as their social-ization, education, and exposure to technologies, their learning styles can help them to catch-up.

Personality Traits. Many risk-taking individuals find it difficult to adapt to a computer's discipline. On the other hand, many people with congenital disabilities who were socialized to be quiet and passive often adapt to the computer's structure much more easily and willingly. This, too, is an area where being a women may have benefit!

Judgment and Preference. Many persons prefer to use a personal care attendant or what they themselves have, however limited, as opposed to a mechanical replacement for their limited functions. They want the "human touch" and actively strive to "not look different." Additionally, consumers can differ in their judgments of the potential functional gains assistive devices offer them, as the following quote from a woman rehabilitation professional indicates:

> One person with cerebral palsy, for example, may determine that a device will not improve her speech intelligibility enough to warrant its use, while another equally affected individual may see a device as not only desirable, but indispensable. I am working with a person now who found her own balance. She has made very effective use of a small, portable, communica-tion device by using it to augment a word here and there.

Adjustment and Outlook. Factors affecting a person's outlook include depression and pessimism arising from the process of adjust-ment to a disability. People with disabilities attach different meanings to what has happened to them and what their future is likely to be like. Pre-existing temperament and ways of coping are just two factors that can influence the length and quality of the recovery and rehabilitation process and adjustment.

Individuals who use assistive devices say that they have goals they want to pursue, believe obstacles to their independence can be overcome, tend to focus on expanding their capabilities, see opportunities rather than limitations and believe they control their quality of life. Device users are not easily discouraged; in fact, they enjoy challenge. As noted by a former director of a rehabilitation unit who is now the director of a medical division for a large corporation:

> It appears that assistive device use depends on the person's decision that (1) he or she was going to perform a given task and (2) that it could not be done without a device. Often, time, learning, doing, and yearning is necessary before that decision is made. Systems (and people) which force the decision on the person prematurely are flawed.

Attending to and monitoring the self-esteem of the client is important in the timing of assistive technology recommendations. Assistive technology use requires an admission to the self that one cannot, and possibly never will, do a functional task on one's own. It requires admitting a loss, weakness, or deficit and this can be distressing. A push for premature device use can be a mistake for those individuals who, as one person has said, "first need time to get used to just the thought of it."

CHARACTERISTICS OF THE TECHNOLOGY AND SERVICE DELIVERY

A woman with one or two hearing aids, or with a communication system, is "ego involved" to an extent different from one with an "impersonal" environmental control system and levels of comfort with use, even around family members, vary widely. Feelings of being conspicuous are compounded when assistive technologies are designed to look functional and utilitarian for funding sources and, as a result, leave many women feeling deviant and stigmatized.

Assistive technologies are not used if other support services are not there. For example, a specially-equipped van is less useful when there are no handicapped parking spaces. Homebound persons (such as some elderly people) and those in remote and rural areas, may be unfamiliar with many devices because they may not have access to peers or trained professionals to help them learn to use them properly. Training in device use is very important, as one woman noted, for *everyone*:

> The technology itself requires *a lot* of training. Not only to train the user, but the caregivers because the caregivers have to learn how to problem-solve if there's a sudden malfunction of the equipment. We also need to start training those informal technicians, such as the neighborhood electrician, who are called upon to fabricate and trouble-shoot with devices.

All assistive technologies, but especially the "non-essential" ones, might achieve higher utilization rates by women if more female users were available as role models. Peer modeling and support is not only important in presenting assistive technologies as options to individuals, but in learning adaptive behaviors in general and for the development of self-confidence and a positive identity.

Finally, counseling services need to be (re)incorporated into comprehensive rehabilitation programs in order to discuss and work through feelings, attitudes, and fears that interfere with rehabilitation. Counseling specialists, trained to have an interactive, comprehensive and interdisciplinary approach to problem intervention, can "look at the whole picture." They can help people resolve identity confusion and come to terms with and enhance their own unique circumstances. Counselors can also educate and provide support to other members of the rehabilitation team. There is currently a big need for rehabilitation engineers to have support in the human services they deliver. While educated for technical careers, they increasingly find themselves in the position of needing to provide more psychosocial interventions. These highly motivated and relatively new additions to the comprehensive rehabilitation team merit increased attention to their unique roles.

CONCLUSION

Devices make possible negative as well as positive changes for women with disabilities. Technology alone is rarely the answer to a person's enhanced quality of life. Assistive technologies can help a woman access more opportunities and exercise more options, but they require support services and training, attention to the person's basic needs, personality, preferences, and capabilities and the characteristics of the milieu in which the device will be used.

When recommending a device for a person's use, it is crucial to assess strengths as well as limitations, evaluate the existence of ancillary limitations (such as low vision for the user of a device with a graphic display), select the most cost efficient device that is the best ergonomic and aesthetic match, provide training in use and maintenance, and follow-up to determine the extent to which the device is meeting the consumer's needs and determine any secondary effects it may have presented. By keeping in mind (a) the characteristics of the environment or milieu in which the device will be used, (b) the person's personality and preferences, (c) and the capabilities and characteristics of the technology under consideration, the recommendation will, thus, emerge from that person's unique needs and will be consumer-driven.

One consideration of such great importance that it requires special emphasis is the active involvement of the user in the decision-making process. Too often, women with disabilities are excluded from decisions regarding assistive technologies and other matters which affect their lives. This perpetuates the belief that women with disabilities are passive and incompetent.

Some tough, but important, questions that should be asked of every individual considering the purchase or adoption of any assistive technology are:

1. What do you–not someone else–think you need?
2. What is it exactly that makes you think that? What's led you to that decision or opinion?
3. Please describe one of your typical days, from the time you get up to the time you go to bed at night, including your activities, the people you usually see, the places you go.

4. Describe what you *wish* a typical day will be like one year
   from now. Five years and ten years from now.
5. What do you see as being most useful and helpful to you
   now? In the future in achieving your goals?

When the answers to these five questions suggest assistive
technology use, then the next series of questions should ask:

6. What do you want to *do*?
7. Where? In what different environments or settings?
8. What assistance is already available in those settings? What
   will assistive technology use add to–or take away from–that
   assistance?
9. What changes in lifestyle are involved? For whom?
10. What non-technical solutions are available? What are the pros
    and cons to them?
11. What's the lowest level technical solution that will meet your
    needs and achieve the goal?
12. How well is it functioning in the various situations where you
    use it?

Above all, realize that the purpose of an assistive technology is to
enhance a person's functioning and quality of life and if the device
doesn't do that, it will not be used.

While rehabilitation engineering settings are very responsive to
the physical needs of women with disabilities, there is frequently
less attention given to the psychological and social aspects of assistive device use. By consulting a model such as the *MPT Model* (see
Appendix B), the need for a potential intervention is flagged so that
an initial profile suggesting non-use can be changed to one favoring
use. This will reduce device abandonment, decrease premature or
inappropriate device recommendations, and help assure that those
individuals who can most benefit from a device will receive and use
it. Documentation of the initial and post-intervention profiles can:
(a) help provide the rationale for funding a device or training for
that device, (b) demonstrate an individual's improvement in functioning over time, and (c) help organize information typifying the
needs of a state's or facility's clientele.

REFERENCES

American Association of University Women (AAUW). (1992). *The AAUW report: How schools shortchange girls.* Washington, D.C.: Author.

Gilligan, C. (1982). *In a different voice: Psychological theory and women's development.* Cambridge, Mass.: Harvard University Press.

Littrell, J.L. (1991). Women with disabilities in community college computer training programs. In H. Murphy (Ed.), *Proceedings of the Sixth Annual Conference, Technology and Persons with Disabilities* (pp. 553-562), California State University, Northridge.

Scherer, M.J. (1992). *The Health Care Technology Predisposition Assessment (HCT PA),* Rochester, NY. (Available from Marcia J. Scherer, Rochester Inst. of Technology, 1 Lomb Memorial Drive, Rochester, NY 14623).

Scherer, M.J., & McKee, B.G. (1989). *The Assistive Technology Device Predisposition Assessment (ATD PA),* Rochester, NY.

Scherer, M.J., & McKee, B.G. (1991). *The Workplace Technology Predisposition Assessment (WT PA),* Rochester, NY.

Scherer, M.J., McKee, B.G. & Young, M.A. (1990). *The Educational Technology Predisposition Assessment (ET PA).* Rochester, NY.

Scherer, M.J., & Weissberger, R.M. (1989). *The Technology Overload Assessment (TOA).* Rochester, NY.

Assistive Technology Influences

	Milieu	Personality	Technology
U S E **Optimal**	Support from family/peers/ employer Realistic expectations of family/ employer Setting/environment fully supports and rewards use	Proud to use device Motivated Cooperative Optimistic Good coping skills Patient Self-disciplined Generally positive life experiences Has the skills to use the device Perceives discrepancy between desired and current situation	Goal achieved with no pain, fatigue or stress Compatible with/enhances the use of other technologies Is safe, reliable, easy to use and maintain Has the desired transportability No better options currently available
Partial/ Reluctant	Pressure for use from either family/peers/employer Assistance often not available Setting/environment discourages use or makes use awkward	Embarrassed to use device Unmotivated Impatient/impulsive Unrealistic expectations Low self-esteem Somewhat intimidated by technology Technology partially or occasionally fits with lifestyle Deficits in skills needed for use	Goal not fully achieved or with discomfort/strain Requires a lot of set-up Interferes somewhat with the use of other technologies Device is inefficient Other options to device use exist

N			
O	**Avoidance**	Lack of support from either family/peers/employer Unrealistic expectations of others Assistance not available Setting/environment disallows or prevents use	Person doesn't want it Embarrassed to use device Depressed Unmotivated Uncooperative Withdrawn Intimidated by technology Many changes required in lifestyle Does not have skills for use	*Perceived* lack of goal achievement or too much strain/discomfort in use Requires a lot of set-up Perceived or determined to be incompatible with the use of other technologies Too expensive Long delay for delivery Other options to device use exist
N			
U			
S	**Abandonment**	Lack of support from either family/peers/employer Setting/environment discourages or makes use awkward Requires assistance that is not available	Embarrassed to use device Depressed Low self-esteem Hostile/angry Withdrawn Resistant Poor socialization and coping skills Many changes in lifestyle with device use Lacks skills to use device and training is not available	Goal not achieved and/or discomfort/strain in use Is incompatible with the use of other technologies Has been outgrown Is difficult to use Device is inefficient Repairs/service not timely or affordable Other options to use became available
E			

Appendix B

Two assistive technology assessment/screening instruments were developed to assure that: (a) Consumer input would drive the *Matching Person and Technology* (*MPT*) process, (b) the degree of match between consumer and professional perspectives could be assessed, (c) professionals are guided into considering all relevant influences on device use while focusing primarily on the consumer's quality of life, (d) other professionals and consumers could verify the existence and importance of the influences on assistive technology use that emerged from this research, and (e) possible mismatches between a proposed technology and a potential user could be flagged to reduce non-use or inappropriate use of assistive technologies and the disappointment and frustration that often accompanies less than ideal use.

The two assessment instruments are *The Assistive Technology Device Predisposition Assessment* (*ATD PA*) consumer and professional versions (Scherer & McKee, 1989), which are designed to be used as a set. An *Educational Technology Predisposition Assessment* (*ET PA*) (Scherer, McKee & Young, 1990), *Workplace Technology Predisposition Assessment* (*WT PA*) (Scherer & McKee, 1991), *Health Care Technology Predisposition Assessment* (*HCT PA*) (Scherer, 1992) and *Technology Overload Assessment* (Scherer & Weissberger, 1989) are also available. All instruments have a checklist format and are situational. They are currently in pilot form and are undergoing further refinement as information concerning their usefulness is collected across the U.S. and abroad. Preliminary analyses indicate that they have good inter-rater reliability and criterion-related validity (since the items emerged from the actual experiences of users and non-users, they have content validity).

An Open Letter to Health and Mental Health Care Professionals from a Survivor of Sexual Exploitation

Martha E. Sheldon

SUMMARY. The following is a personal account from a woman who has cerebral palsy dealing with her experiences with sexual exploitation. The article gives helpful suggestions to the mental and health care profession about working with a survivor of sexual abuse who happens to have a disability.

I am writing this as a mental health professional, a survivor of sexual exploitation, and a woman who happens to have cerebral palsy. In many ways my social work training has been a great asset in my recovery. Many people who are disabled are not as lucky. I am writing this to make the health and mental health profession aware of the emotional needs of the disabled who are also survivors of sexual exploitation.

At this point in my recovery process, as a survivor of incest I am

Martha Sheldon, MSW, has a Master's Degree in Social Work from Barry University, Miami, FL. She is a part-time consultant to a private rehabilitation firm based in Miami, FL.

Correspondence may be addressed to: Martha E. Sheldon, 13570 SW 156 Lane #C, Miami, FL 33177.

[Haworth co-indexing entry note]: "An Open Letter to Health and Mental Health Care Professionals from a Survivor of Sexual Exploitation." Sheldon, Martha E.. Co-published simultaneously in *Women & Therapy* (The Haworth Press, Inc.) Vol. 14, No. 3/4, 1993, pp. 133-137; and: *Women with Disabilities: Found Voices* (ed: Mary E. Willmuth, and Lillian Holcomb) The Haworth Press, Inc., 1993, pp. 133-137. Multiple copies of this article/chapter may be purchased from The Haworth Document Delivery Center [1-800-3-HAWORTH; 9:00 a.m. - 5:00 p.m. (EST)].

ready to deal with my anger. It took many years to get to this point. Besides working through the feelings of being raped twice by the same man, and getting into relationships with men where the only thing the men were interested in was going to bed, I also had an incestuous relationship with my father. Once I became aware that it was wrong for any man to violate my body and psyche I continued to have problems with harassment to the point of being abused verbally and physically.

Not until my mid-twenties, on my own, and in my last year of graduate school did I become aware that I *was* a sexual person. At the time I was having trouble adjusting to the "real world." Therefore, I went to a mental health counselor who helped me realize that I was a person, who happened to be a woman, who just happened to have cerebral palsy. Also I participated in a woman's awareness group. There, I learned that I had sexual needs, wants, and desires.

About three or four months before I went into therapy I called the county for a bus schedule. The man who answered the phone asked me my name, address, and would I like to go out with him. I said, "yes." The next thing I know, he showed up at my door. He said he wanted to "*FUCK*" before we went out. I did not want to. But to please him, I had intercourse with him. Besides, I wanted to go on a *REAL* date. After he had an orgasm, he left, without saying a word. I did not know what had happened. I knew I did not like it. Although inside I was angry I didn't do anything.

About five months after I went to the counselor, the same man knocked on the door one night and told me he wanted to take me out. But first he wanted to "*FUCK ME*." Again, I did not want to. But I wanted to please him. I wanted to go out! We had sex on the living room floor. After he reached orgasm, he went into the bathroom, put his clothes on, and walked out the door.

After he left, I got angry. This time I realized he had violated my body as well as my psyche. When I became aware of what he had done, I called a friend, who came over, and together we called the police. The police said it was not rape because I let the guy in and consented to a sexual act.

Now with the professional background I have, I know it was rape, because I had tremendous gaps in my psycho/social/sexual development. This meant that, although intellectually I was an adult, socially and emotionally I was functioning at a much lower level. This was because I did not go through the typical adolescent development regarding interacting with the opposite sex.

Slowly, my family found out. Except for my father who wanted to kill the man, the rape was never discussed. It took me several years of therapy to realize it was not my fault I was raped.

Two days after I was raped, I was taken to the Rape Treatment Center. The doctor was uncomfortable with my disability. He kept on asking my friends what had happened. It was *ME*, not them, that was raped. Fortunately, my friends did not do my talking for me.

It was during this period of time that I began to have relationships with four or five men, both men with disabilities and able-bodied men. I wanted to go out on dates. But most dates ended up in bed. I did not enjoy it. I went along with it because I thought I had to. It never occured to me to say *"NO!"*

Since I was four, whenever I would become angry, I would become self-destructive. On several occasions I have broken phones and a radio or two. For years I did not understand why. I needed to feel the physical pain to let go of the anger.

I could not get angry at another person, I got angry at myself and physically abused myself. At points in my life the anger and the pain have been so great I have wanted to die. On numerous occasions I have attempted suicide.

It was not until two months after a suicide attempt that I began to become aware of the cause of the problem. I had trouble with men and that was connected to the self-abusive tendencies and the suicidal thoughts.

I did not know where it came from, but I found myself listening to a very graphic, explicit book, a recording for talking books. The book had several stories about father and daughter incestuous relationships. After reading the book, I knew *IT* happened to me. My father went to bed with me. I told my psychiatrist what had happened. I told him about the book and the faint feelings from the past when my father went to bed with me. Part of me wanted to deny it. But inside, I knew it happened.

The denial of the incestuous relationship lasted for many years. Now I accept that it did take place. The memories are vague. I blocked them from my consciousness. There are several things I do remember about the relationship. I do not remember having intercourse with my father. But I do remember him fondling my breasts and genitalia. He was always drunk when he did it.

I remember the last time he got drunk and went to bed with me. I was in my mid twenties. The next morning I went to my mother and said, "Mommy, Mommy, Guess what?" "Daddy went to bed with me." My mother's mouth dropped open and she said, "Oh!" The only other time *IT* was mentioned was during one of the first television specials on incest.

Although I graduated from college, it never dawned on me that going to bed with my father was wrong. I knew I did not like it. But I was taught to do everything my parents told me to do. The only time I told anyone else was my roommate who was my best friend at a residential school. At the time we were in our teens. The subject was never mentioned at the institution. One day we were talking about the taboo subject, and I asked her if she went to bed with her father. She said "yes." So we thought it was normal for fathers to go to bed with their daughters.

Looking back as a survivor of sexual exploitation I realize that if I had had knowledge about sexuality, known what my rights were as a sexual person, that I could choose the type of relationship I wanted, and that I had the right to say "NO," I would have been in control of my life. However, the empowerment of knowing my rights does not make me immune to sexual exploitation. I am dependent on others for certain needs. It is very difficult to tell the authorities that your rights have been violated knowing that you are not going to be believed or even worse, that retribution will occur.

That is exactly what happened to me once when I reported a driver who drove for a transportation service for the disabled sponsored by the county. The driver touched my breasts and told me "how big they grew." Earlier on numerous occasions the same driver would get out of his car and urinate in front of my apartment or where I worked (which was a children's psychiatric hospital). I kept on reporting the urination incidents to the County. Nothing was ever done.

So when I reported the incident where the driver touched my breast I reported it to the county. Also, I filed a complaint with the police. Nothing ever came of the investigation. But because I made the authorities aware of the incidents, the driver told the other drivers his story. Needless to say, I was not very popular with the other drivers. One driver went so far as to abuse me verbally and physically.

In closing I would like to say it has taken me years to become aware that I am a survivor of many types of sexual exploitation. I have come to terms with the unsuccessful relationships, the two rapes, and the retribution. The little girl inside cannot understand why the man (my father) who used to be my only connection with the outside world (i.e., the only person who took me places) would hurt his little girl. It has been hard to find therapists to work with me on the incest issue. When they did try to confront me on the issue I turned the anger inward. Even though therapists have been well meaning, I would like to offer the following advice:

1. Incest is the issue, *not* the disability.
2. Studies show that most incest survivors are children of alcoholics, but very few mental health professionals are aware that there is a high rate of alcoholism/chemical dependency among parents of disabled children. Thus, there is probably a high rate of sex abuse in those families.
3. This can be applied to able-bodied as well as incest survivors with disabilities. Do not make any judgments about self destructive behaviors. It just confirms that they are *BAD*. In the past when I felt self destructive, it helped when I told a trusted, non-judgmental person that I felt like hurting myself and an agreement was made *NOT* to hurt myself for a specific period of time.
4. Do not expect incest survivors to deal with the issue and then feel "better." Some can and, that is great. For others, like me, it is an on-going process.

Sexually Abused Women with Mental Retardation: Hidden Victims, Absent Resources

Marilyn M. Stromsness

SUMMARY. The aims of this report were to provide a description of sexual abuse among adult women with mild mental retardation and to examine the characteristics and experiences of the sexual abuse among these adults.

Data collected in a 55-item structured interview from fourteen, predominantly Caucasian women in a community based, non-clinical population, were used to achieve the aims of the report.

Nearly 82% of survivors were molested prior to their 18th birthday. Sex education appeared not to prevent abuse, but instead appeared to increase the reporting of sexual abuse. The vast majority of survivors received no medical, psychological, or legal help.

The conclusion to be drawn from this report is that barriers are effectively erected which prevent women with mental retardation, who are also survivors of sexual abuse, access to the same essential therapeutic intervention non-retarded women possess.

Marilyn Stromsness, PhD, is a registered psychologist at Xanthos, Inc. (a family therapy agency) in Alameda, California, where she is completing her postdoctoral fellowship. In 1981, Dr. Stromsness founded the first self-help support group in the Midwest for adult survivors of incest and since that time she has pursued her interest in family sexual abuse.

Correspondence may be addressed to: Marilyn Stromsness, PhD, 3230 Storer Ave., Oakland, CA 94619.

Marilyn Stromsness gratefully acknowledges the assistance of Carol Huffine, PhD, in the preparation of this manuscript.

[Haworth co-indexing entry note]: "Sexually Abused Women with Mental Retardation: Hidden Victims, Absent Resources." Stromsness, Marilyn M. Co-published simultaneously in *Women & Therapy* (The Haworth Press, Inc.) Vol. 14, No. 3/4, 1993, pp. 139-152; and: *Women with Disabilities: Found Voices* (ed: Mary E. Willmuth, and Lillian Holcomb) The Haworth Press, Inc., 1993, pp. 139-152. Multiple copies of this article/chapter may be purchased from The Haworth Document Delivery Center [1-800-3-HAWORTH; 9:00 a.m. - 5:00 p.m. (EST)].

139

The purpose of this report is to provide a description of sexual abuse among adult women with mental retardation using data collected in interviews with a community based, non-clinical population.

Today, one out of every three American females and one out of every seven American males are at risk of being sexually abused before reaching eighteen years of age (Bass & Davis, 1988). However, it is estimated that people with mental retardation are sexually abused four times more often than the non-retarded (Kempton & Stanfield, 1988). Some writers have suggested that 70% to 99% of people with developmental delay are sexually abused by their eighteenth birthday (Baladerian, 1985; Hard, 1987; Ryerson, 1984; Summers, 1987). Relative to the estimates of extraordinarily high rates of sexual abuse of the population with retardation, the number of sexual abuse cases that get reported is minuscule (Senn, 1988), and we know little about the circumstance of the abuse experienced by those with mental retardation.

According to the American Psychiatric Association, one percent of the population has mental retardation. Chamberlain, Rauh, Passer, McGrath, and Burket (1984) state that the mildly retarded, who constitute 85% of the population with retardation (American Psychiatric Association 1987), are the most vulnerable to sexual abuse.

Documenting the prevalence of sexual abuse among adults with mild mental retardation and investigating the characteristics associated with their sexual abuse would provide the data needed to document the need for: (a) expanded resources and services, (b) early implementation of sexual abuse avoidance curricula, and (c) training programs for care providers and helping professionals who could effectively intervene to protect those with mental retardation from sexual abuse or its damaging effects.

METHOD

Sample

The sampling pool consisted of 359 adults with mild mental retardation who had the ability to give informed consent (determined by their case managers), and who had expressive and receptive language skills, basic knowledge of sexual terms, and who were unconserved. Potential respondents resided in community care facilities, homes of relatives, or lived independently.

Instruments/Measures

The Socio-Sexual Knowledge and Attitude Test (SSKAT), designed by Wish, McCombs, and Edmonson (1980), was administered to assess respondents' knowledge of sexual terminology and to elicit the words they used for body parts and sexual activity. The respondent's terminology was recorded and used throughout the interview.

Structured Interview

An interview schedule consisting of 55 open-ended questions was developed for this study. It includes questions about (a) demographic data and social characteristics, (b) sexual knowledge, (c) attitudes toward crime, (d) experiences of sexual abuse and other crimes, (e) aftermath and effect of reporting sexual abuse, and (f) feelings about being victimized.

Procedures

Letters describing the study and response cards were mailed to the 359 unconserved adults with mild mental retardation who resided in four San Francisco Bay area counties. Respondents signaled their interest in the study by returning the post card. Phone contacts were made with potential respondents who were then given more detailed information about the study. If they were still willing to participate, an appointment was arranged for a confidential and private one-hour interview.

RESULTS

Subjects

Of the 359 recruitment letters sent, seven were returned because of incorrect addresses. Thirty-eight postcards were returned indicating that potential subjects could be called and told more about the study. From the 38 post-cards that were returned, 27 interviews were scheduled. This resulted in a final sample size of seven-and-one-half percent of the pool.

As Table 1 shows, just over half of the subjects were female, seventy-four percent grew up in their family homes, two-thirds were over the age of 30 years, almost 90% were Caucasian, and overall, the respondents' general knowledge of sexual body parts and their functions and of sexual behavior was very good.

Of the 14 female subjects, just under 80% of them had been sexually abused at least once by the time of the interview. Of these latter women, 82% currently live in a board and care home; none of the women who had not been molested currently lived in a board and care home. Because only three women make up the non-abuse group, it is impossible to test this difference for statistical significance.

Sex education and sexual abuse status are presented in Table 2. All of the non-sexually abused women and 82% of the sexually abused women reported having received some form of formal sex education. However forty-five percent of the sexually abused and 67% of the non-abused had received that education prior to reaching their 21st birthday.

Together, eleven women reported 59 separate instances of sexual abuse (seven men reported 22 separate instances of sexual abuse). Frequency was asked about but not reported because of vagueness of the typical response (e.g., a lot, all the time). The sexual abuse experiences were divided into those that involved sexual contact, defined as intercourse (anal, oral, vaginal), fondling, or forced masturbation and those that did not involve sexual contact. Non-contact abuse included being forced to view pornography or to pose for nude pictures, being watched while undressing, and having the offender expose his or her genitals. For females, 71% of the sexual molestations described here involved sexual contact (for males, 50% involved sexual contact).

The largest group of offenders in this study comprised acquaintances and relatives. Forty-six percent of the sexually abused women reported incestuous experiences (defined as sexual abuse by biological, adopted, step, or foster family members).

Table 1

Demographic characteristics of 27 mildly mentally
retarded adults by gender and abuse status

	Sexually Abused			
	Yes		No	
	Female	Male	Female	Male
	N	N	N	N
Gender	11	7	3	6
Age				
< 30	3	3	1	2
30-39	5	2	2	1
40-49	3	2	-	1
> 50	-	-	-	2
Total	11	7	3	6
Ethnicity				
Caucasian	11	6	3	4
Other	-	1	-	2
Total	11	7	3	6
Growing Up				
Family home	9	6	3	2
Combination home & institution	2	1	-	4
Total	11	7	3	6
Current Residency				
Own Apartment	2	2	2	1
Family Home	-	3	1	2
Board & Care Home	9	2	-	3
Total	11	7	3	6
Employed				
Yes	9	6	3	4
No	2	1	-	2
Total	11	7	3	6

TABLE 1 (continued)

	Sexually Abused			
	Yes		No	
	Female	Male	Female	Male
	N	N	N	N
Significant Relationship				
Married	1	1	-	-
Dating	7	5	1	2
Neither	3	1	2	4
Total	11	7	3	6 .

Table 2

Positive Sex education and abuse status

	Sexual Abuse	
	Yes	No
Sex Education		
Yes	9	3
No	2	-
Total	11	3
Age of Sex Education		
< 21	5	2
> 21	4	1
No sex education	2	-
Total	11	3
Age of Molestation(s)		
< 21	2	-
21 +	2	-
Combination	7	-
Total	11	-

Of the incidents involving relatives and acquaintances, 68% involved sexual contact, while 75% of the abuse by strangers involved sexual contact (among the men, 47% of the incestuous incidents and 80% of the abuse by strangers involved sexual contact).

Effects of the Abuse

When asked "did the sexual molestation upset you a lot or not very much," the overwhelming majority responded "a lot." Some of the sexually abused women were ambivalent about the effects of their victimization. For instance, one respondent whose father molested her for 30 years and ended with his death when she was 45 years old, had this to say:

> He would first give me a bath, then he'd dry me off and play sex with me. I did learn a lot from all of it. If it wasn't for my dad, I would never have learned how to bathe a penis. But I didn't enjoy it. I don't think it was a very good thing done to me. Dad told me he loved me. I turned him down a lot, but he was still sexual with me most every day. It was his way of showing love, but I think it was wrong. His mind might have been a little off.

Although this women wept the entire time, she insisted on telling her story, since as she put it, "I've never told anyone before."

Reporting the Abuse

Two of the women who were sexually abused did not tell anyone about any of their victimizations (43% of the men never told). The abusers' requests that they "promise not to tell" silenced 64% of the women for at least some period of time, and two respondents were paid to keep quiet, one with cash and one with cigarettes. Of the women who reported their molestation(s), 46% told more than one person or told more than once. Of the persons who were told, 59% were mandatory reporters, meaning that they were members of the helping professions (teachers, physicians, foster parents, social workers, etc.) which are required by law to report cases of suspected abuse of dependent adults.

The Effects of Telling

In only two instances did "telling" result in some kind of legal action. In one case the respondent's testimony was disregarded as the judge allegedly had difficulty understanding her. The other respondent's foster brother was sentenced to four years in prison. Two of the abused women were seen by medical personnel, and five of the eleven women (including 45% of those who experienced some form of contact abuse) received some form of counseling as a result of sexual abuse. Counseling ranged from one appointment to bi-monthly sessions over the course of one year.

Self-Perceived Vulnerability

The data suggest that women feel more vulnerable to other forms of crime than to sexual abuse. For example, 71% of the women felt that crime happens a lot to people with mental retardation, but when the crime was sexual abuse, the proportion of women who thought it happened a lot dropped to 57%. However, when asked if they personally were afraid of being sexually abused, 8 of the 11 abused women (and two of the three non-abused women) replied positively. Nine of the victimized (and two of the non-victimized) had developed strategies to prevent sexual abuse. These strategies ranged from safeguards such as avoiding risky situations or persons and keeping their doors locked to irrelevant acts like using birth control techniques.

At least half of the respondents had opinions about why people commit crimes against the mentally retarded and the theme of special vulnerability was common. Responses included: "because they know they can knock the shit out of us," "because mentally retarded people might not be able to defend themselves," and "because of our disability they feel we're not normal or capable of doing what they can, but sometimes we can, even better." One very forthright person, who not only felt vulnerable to sexual abuse but unprotected by the system, had this to say: "They figure a person who is handicapped with retardation is not going to testify or even tell and anyway if they did tell, the system would just ignore the complaint because this person is retarded or handicapped."

DISCUSSION

It is commonly believed that the idea of having sex with a person with mental retardation is repulsive and that no one would ever take advantage of the vulnerable retarded population (Cole, 1986). Yet, this community-based study yielded results consistent with clinical studies showing that a very large portion of women with mental retardation have experienced sexual abuse. Most of the sexual abuse was contact rather than non-contact sexual abuse and only 45% of the more seriously abused received some counseling.

Is it the disability of mental retardation itself or the lack of social/sexual knowledge that makes the person vulnerable to sexual abuse (Senn, 1988)? Craft and Craft (1983) suggested that, among other things, it is compliancy that often makes adults with mental retardation perfect victims of sexual abuse. In addition, women with mental retardation (a) often have poor social judgement, (b) depend on other adults for care, (c) are easily persuaded and made to feel guilty through enticement or entrapment, (d) often live socially isolated lives, (e) are emotionally deprived, (f) lack the necessary social/sexual education to distinguish between appropriate or exploitive behavior, or to avoid sexual abuse, (g) are more likely to trust strangers, (h) have difficulty judging the motivation behind other people's behavior, (i) demonstrate and receive affection more freely, and (j) often lack the ability to defend themselves. It is easy to see why, if a sex offender has a choice between a retarded or non-retarded victim, the offender's choice frequently will be a person with mental retardation (Longo, 1981). Of particular concern for women with mental retardation is that they often place themselves in a high risk situation in order to obtain a male companion. In addition to all the reasons mentioned above, women with mental retardation tend to place a higher than usual value on having a boyfriend. Thus, they will compromise themselves rather than risk the loss of a lover, even if that lover exploits and abuses them.

As with the mainstream population, gender plays a role in sexual abuse of people with mental retardation. In this study 79% of the female and 54% of the male respondents reported being sexually molested.

Not only are those with mental retardation more vulnerable to sexual exploitation than the mainstream population, once exploited they have limited access to the resources that are provided for non-retarded people (Moglia, 1986; Rosen, 1983). In spite of the estimated high incidence of sexual abuse among people with mental retardation, the number of helping professionals trained to provide psychotherapy to mentally retarded victims of sexual abuse remains small. In fact, this author's informal, but extensive search of Alameda County, California in 1988 yielded no one trained to provide psychotherapy to people with mental retardation who were also survivors of sexual abuse.

The prevention strategies described by the subjects might be somewhat effective in avoiding sexual abuse by strangers on the streets, but in most cases they had been abused by relatives or people with authority over them. As Fisher and Field (1985) have pointed out, people with mental retardation are taught community skills, but are not taught how to protect themselves from the community.

To avoid or report abuse could mean losing the security of a family, leaving the stability of a long-term, board-and-care facility, being fired from a job, or losing a lover. While these costs of reporting are not unique to women with mental retardation, their vulnerability is compounded by their awareness of their lack of resources and the lack of persons trained to help them.

The lack of effective therapeutic intervention has serious implications for those with mental retardation. These implications range from revictimization to themselves becoming offenders and a variety of mental disorders unrelated to mental retardation such as clinical depression, post-traumatic stress disorder, and somatoform disorders. Clinical psychologists and their training schools ethically cannot ignore this population any longer.

Sex education has been promoted as a strategy for the prevention of sexual molestation (Baladerian, 1985; Cruz, Price-Williams, & Andron, 1988; Hard, 1987; Kempton & Stanfield, 1988; O'Day, 1983; Rosen, 1983; Sgroi, 1988; Thornburg, 1985; Watson, 1984). In the present study, sex education had not protected the respondents from sexual abuse. Eighty-two percent of the abused women had received some form of sex education although 55% of them did not receive it till after their 21st birthday (see Table 2).

The results of the present study suggest that at least two aspects of sex education, timing and content, need closer attention. For example, although one half of the women received sex education before their twenty-first birthday, 64% of the women were, nevertheless, molested before turning 21 years of age. In addition, the role of assertiveness training in conjunction with socio-sexual education should be effectively evaluated. Because of their developmental delays, many women with mental retardation are unable to translate information into action and to generalize what they learn in the safety of the classroom to the environments in which they are victimized. Sgroi (1989) suggests that self-confidence, obtained from opportunities to carry out that which they can freely articulate, might help people with mental retardation to protect themselves.

Originally the primary purpose of this study was epidemiological. I wanted to access the prevalence of sexual abuse in a non-clinical population, hoping thereby to understand the differences between estimated and reported cases of sexual abuse among adults with mild mental retardation.

Because of the low response rate, that goal could not be achieved. The low response rate is the result largely of numerous obstacles encountered in the subject recruitment process.

From early on, it was clear that the biggest obstacle to this study was the system designed to help those with mental retardation; it very effectively stands between potential investigators and the adult with mild mental retardation. Staff at one regional center agreed to consider cooperating with me only if I agreed to: (a) eliminate questions about reporting abuse to case managers, case managers' levels of compliance with mandates to report suspected cases of client sexual abuse, and case managers' investigation and follow up on reports of sexual abuse, and (b) have subjects waive any financial obligation by the regional center should they admit to being sexually abused and in need of psychotherapy.

The director of another regional center embraced the research and was willing to cooperate in any way as long as the state agency with authority over regional centers approved the research proposal. The assistant director of the state agency claimed to support the intent of the study, but was unable to support the project because:

(a) the study might retraumatize the subjects by awakening nascent memories of past abuse, (b) participation might provoke additional abuse, and (c) no resources were available to mitigate the trauma or end the abuse.

In spite of the concerns of the assistant director, the study ultimately was approved but with restrictions that probably impeded recruitment. For instance, I did not have access to administrators of public board and care homes. Past experiences suggested that "hands-on" administrators would have been willing to facilitate the research.

In this study, only unconserved adults were sought. This was done not only to circumvent the need for parental permission and agency involvement, but to recognize the autonomy of the unconserved mentally retarded adult. The term "unconserved" would suggest that the persons sought for this study have the same rights as other adults in society, but this, in fact, is not true. As the recruitment process revealed, there is an elaborate system that works to limit the decisions the unconserved mentally retarded adult may make. The limits are justified as ways to protect vulnerable people. As a society, we are caught in the dilemma of wanting those with mental retardation to be as normal as possible, yet we know they are not.

Berstein (1985) suggested that this protective behavior often reflects society's fear and anxiety and not that of the retarded. Aiding and abetting this protectionistic system are relatives and acquaintances, many of whom are the abusers, who erect barriers that make it impossible to figure out the therapeutic needs of women with mental retardation.

Suggestions have been made that the bureaucratic structures described above also impede efforts to intervene when women with mental retardation are victims of sexual abuse (Cruz et al., 1988). Thus, as we try to protect women who are recognized as vulnerable from being taken advantage of in a wide variety of ways, we do not allow them to make decisions for themselves as fully functioning members of society. The inconsistency in this behavior resonates with the respondents' feelings about themselves as women who do not have rights and who know they are vulnerable. Although many women in general feel disenfranchised, these feelings are often exacerbated for women with mental retardation.

The conclusion to be drawn from the foregoing is that it is virtually impossible to obtain a reasonably large and representative sample unless one works from inside the system. Without mandatory cooperation, data will be limited and without the data, it is quite impossible to develop effective strategies to help women with mental retardation learn to protect themselves against sexual abuse or to develop effective therapeutic interventions for women who are sexually abused.

Mental retardation, coupled with exploitive sexual experiences, is an excellent example of double jeopardy. The lack of access to socio-sexual avoidance education, legal resources, and psychological services is inexcusable. It is an unethical society that fails to provide women with mental retardation the same fundamental rights that non-disabled women enjoy.

REFERENCES

American Psychiatric Association. (1987). *Diagnostic and statistical manual of mental disorders* (3rd ed.-revised). Washington, DC: Author.

Baladerian, N.J. (1985). *Prevention of sexual exploitation of developmentally disabled adults.* Paper presented at the 1985 Convention Association of Post-Secondary Educators of the Disabled, Sacramento, California.

Bass, E., & Davis, L. (1988). *The courage to heal.* New York: Harper & Row.

Berstein, N. R. (1985). Sexuality in mentally retarded adolescents. *Medical Aspects of Human Sexuality, 19,* 50-61.

Chamberlain, A., Rauh, J., Passer, A., McGrath, M., & Burket, O. (1984). Issues in fertility control for mentally retarded female adolescents: I. Sexual activity, sexual abuse, and contraception. *Pediatrics, 73,* 445-450.

Cole, S. S. (1986). Facing the challenges of sexual abuse in persons with disabilities. *Sexuality and Disability, 7,* 71-88.

Craft, A., & Craft, M. (Eds.). (1983). *Sex education and counselling for mentally handicapped people.* Kent, England: Costello.

Cruz, V.K., Price-Williams, D., & Andron, L. (1988). Developmentally disabled women who were molested as children. *Social Casework, 69,* 411-419.

Fisher, G.L. & Field, S.L. (1985). Self-protection for persons with disabilities. Development and validation of a skills curriculum. *Career Development for Exceptional Individuals. 8,* 7-16.

Hard, S. (1987). *Sexual abuse of persons with developmental disabilities: A case study.* Unpublished manuscript.

Kempton, W., & Stanfield, J. (1988). *Speaking of sex . . . and persons with special needs* (video). Santa Monica, Ca: James Stanfield and Company.

Longo, R.E. (1981). Sexual assault of handicapped individuals. *Journal of Rehabilitation, 47*, 24-27.

Moglia, R. (1986). Sexual abuse and disability. *Siecus Report, 14*, 9-10.

O'Day, B. (1983). *Preventing sexual abuse of persons with disabilities.* St. Paul: Minnesota Corrections.

Rosen, M. (1983). Sexual exploitation: a community problem. Paper presented at the 7th Symposium of the Committee on the Sexuality of the Developmentally Disabled.

Ryerson, E. (1984). Sexual abuse and self-protection education for developmentally disabled youth: A priority need. *SIECUS Report, 13*, 6-7.

Senn, C.Y. (1988). *Vulnerable: Sexual abuse and people with an intellectual handicap.* Ontario: The G. Allan Roeher Institute.

Sgroi, S.M. (1988). *Vulnerable populations* (Vol. 1). Massachusetts: Lexington.

Sgroi, S.M. (1989). *Vulnerable populations* (Vol. 2). Massachusetts: Lexington.

Summers, C. (1987). *Strong and able: An abuse prevention program for children with disabilities.* San Pablo, CA.: Rape Crisis of West Contra Costa.

Thornburg, H.D. (1985). Sex information as primary prevention. *Journal of sex education and therapy, 11*, 22-27.

Watson, J.D. (1984). Talking about the best kept secret. Sexual abuse and children with disabilities. *The Exceptional Parent, 14*, 15-20.

Wish, J. R., McCombs, K.F., & Edmonson, B. (1980). *Socio-sexual knowledge and attitude test.* Chicago: Stoelting.

Further Labeling Within the Category of Disability Due to Chemical Dependency: Borderline Personality Disorder

Gloria J. Hamilton

SUMMARY. This paper raises issues of validity and consequences of appending the label Borderline Personality Disorder to chemically dependent women who are adult survivors of child sexual abuse. Parallels between documented sequelae of childhood sexual abuse and DSM-III-R delineated characteristics of Borderline Personality Disorder are noted as is the DSM-III-R insertion of "No information" with respect to Predisposing factors. This clinician suggests that the label Borderline Personality Disorder and its accompanying assumptions function to generate negative expectations regarding both the course and direction of the therapy process. By failing to consider the impact of childhood abuse this label provides neither appropriate diagnosis nor therapeutic direction for women with a diagnosis of chemical dependency who are adult survivors of childhood sexual abuse.

Working in a residential chemical dependency treatment program has provided this clinician with opportunity for ongoing assess-

Gloria Hamilton is Assistant Professor of Psychology and works as Clinical Psychologist with Tara Treatment Center for Women with Addictions.

Correspondence may be addressed to: Gloria Hamilton, PhD, Box 87, Department of Psychology, Middle Tennessee State University, Murfreesboro, TN 37132.

[Haworth co-indexing entry note]: "Further Labeling Within the Category of Disability Due to Chemical Dependency: Borderline Personality Disorder." Hamilton, Gloria J. Co-published simultaneously in *Women & Therapy* (The Haworth Press, Inc.) Vol. 14, No. 3/4, 1993, pp. 153-157; and: *Women with Disabilities: Found Voices* (ed: Mary E. Willmuth, and Lillian Holcomb) The Haworth Press, Inc., 1993, pp. 153-157. Multiple copies of this article/chapter may be purchased from The Haworth Document Delivery Center [1-800-3-HAWORTH; 9:00 a.m. - 5:00 p.m. (EST)].

153

ment. This paper is a result of having experience as a psychologist in a residential treatment program for women with addictions. Women who entered the treatment program with a previous diagnosis included women who had been labeled Borderline Personality Disorder. The women so labeled exhibited an unquestioning acceptance of both the diagnosis and accompanying assumptions. On occasion, client responses in initial interview sessions would involve the client's offering her diagnosis both as explanation for current behavior and as expectation of probable inability to change. It appeared that the label functioned to reinforce the client's perception of being personally "flawed," found to be "mentally ill."

As these women continued in treatment, each detailed a history that included at least one incidence of childhood sexual abuse. For many, this was the first time they felt comfortable enough to tell their story; others stated that this was the first time they felt heard and believed. It is an established tenet of this work that the victim of child sexual abuse has both the need and the right to be believed, validated in verbalizing the experience to the care provider, rather than being forced to silence or denial. Client descriptions of past trauma were accompanied by graphic recollections of not having been believed by the persons to whom they turned for protection. The experience of being invalidated, of having one's experience doubted as though the events had never occurred, but were constructed from the mind of a child, further estranged the woman from her own reality.

Client disclosure of past abuse revealed very real, psychologically understandable reasons for exhibiting the behaviors cited by the diagnosticians as meeting the criteria for the label of Borderline Personality Disorder. It is probable that estrangement from one's own reality may result in " . . . marked and persistent identity disturbance . . ." " . . . manifested by uncertainty about several life issues . . ." (American Psychiatric Association, 1987, p. 347), an identifying characteristic of Borderline Personality Disorder.

As the reality of the client was invalidated, her experience became one of powerlessness, leaving her doubting her self, her mental stability, and her worth as someone who should be given support and validation. She was then forced to attempt to cope within the parameters of the reality allowed her. Obviously, she could not

access and work through feelings around experiences that were
ignored or disbelieved by those persons who were "helping" her
deal with her problems. Feelings resulting from the trauma were
denied, resulting in an existence marked by affective instability, a
pattern of affect shift that appears very like diagnostic criteria for
Borderline Personality Disorder.

Psychological phenomena that follow physical escape from trauma include anger that can be triggered by a number of variables,
some of which may appear to the naive observer as inappropriate
stimuli to trigger such intense anger. Anger, sometimes "inappropriate" intense anger, can be a psychological sequela of sexual
abuse. It is also a diagnostic criterion for Borderline Personality
Disorder.

The association between childhood experiences of sexual abuse
and self-damaging behaviors in adulthood has been documented by a
number of researchers. Covington (1982) found 53% of women in
chemical dependency treatment programs reported histories of sexual victimization in childhood. Researchers have also documented the
associations among addictive disorders, finding that persons seldom
enter chemical dependency treatment programs with a single addiction. Miller (1991) found that 80% of alcoholics in chemical dependency treatment populations are dependent on at least one other drug,
usually more. The multiply-addicted include a significant proportion
with behaviors not historically thought of as addictions, such as
eating disorders. Again, psychological sequelae are isomorphic with
diagnostic criteria for Borderline Personality Disorder: "impulsive-
ness in at least two areas that are potentially self-damaging" as in
"substance use, binge eating" (American Psychiatric Association,
1987, p. 347).

It is important to maintain awareness of sociocultural attitudes
and responses both toward the victimized woman and toward the
traumatic event (childhood sexual assault). Social and political attitudes towards victims of sexual assault impact on the diagnostic,
intervention, and recovery process, the politics of these processes
determining what services the victim receives. Social and political
attitudes toward sexual assault have ensured that, for many victims, the
reality of the traumatic event will be disbelieved by significant others
in her life. The impact of this external invalidation process fosters

invalidation of the self as the woman attempts to align with external reality as presented by those who are of importance in her life.

The DSM-III-R manual under the heading of Borderline Personality Disorder records the following:

- Sex ratio. The disorder is more commonly diagnosed in females.
- Prevalence. Borderline Personality Disorder is apparently common.
- Predisposing factors and familial pattern. No information. (American Psychiatric Association, 1987, p. 347).

It is of note that childhood sexual abuse is not mentioned here as a predisposing factor. Surely traumatic events whose psychological sequelae are isomorphic with many, if not all, of the criteria for this disorder would be referenced as possible contributing factors to this diagnosis. The labeling of a person as Borderline Personality Disorder is an event of consequence. The arrival into a chemical dependency treatment program or a mental health facility of a BPD is often heralded with expressions of frustration which acknowledge the difficulties of working with persons labeled Borderline Personality Disorder.

When working with women labeled Borderline Personality Disorder, it is probable that a number of these women are adult survivors of childhood trauma. Certainly, this information would change the therapist's assumptions, perceptions, outcome expectations, and the therapy process.

Therapist attitudes impact on whether the woman will talk with her therapist about the abuse. Therapists can and do influence whether material is even brought up for work, especially by female clients. "I felt like I was making him uncomfortable. So I just didn't talk about it." Women are socialized to recognize and attend to the feelings of others, to "take care of" others and, as the above quote underscores, "others" includes therapists. Clients are sensitive to the comfort level of the therapist and respond accordingly.

The American Psychological Association Task Force for A Women's Mental Health Agenda references descriptive studies that confirm the ". . . alarming numbers of people who are physically and sexually abused and the relative lack of attention given these topics in taking routine psychiatric histories" (Russo, 1985, p. 11). Brodsky and

Hare-Mustin (1980) state, "There is considerable evidence that therapists' knowledge about issues affecting the lives of women is inadequate" (p. 386). It is probable that women with a history of childhood sexual abuse are both overserved (handicapped by an inappropriate label) and underserved by mental health delivery systems. Carmen, Russo, and Miller (1984) explain: "For disorders congruent with sex role stereotypes . . . women show higher rates of service utilization than do men. . . . In contrast, problems of women . . . such as . . . sexual abuse have often been ignored . . . " (p. 35).

Courtois (1988) has presented an effective and reasoned critique of the practice of labeling survivors of childhood sexual abuse with the label of Borderline Personality Disorder. This paper addresses those same concerns and suggests that this label provides neither appropriate diagnosis nor a solid foundation for adequate treatment of the problems these women are dealing with as they attempt to begin the recovery process.

REFERENCES

American Psychiatric Association (1987). *Diagnostic and statistical manual of mental disorders* (3rd ed. revised). Washington, DC: Author.

Brodsky, A. M., & Hare-Mustin, R. (Eds.) (1980). *Women and psychotherapy: An assessment of research and practice*. New York: Guilford Press.

Carmen, E. (H.), Russo, N. F., & Miller, J. B. (1984). Inequality in women's mental health. In P. P. Rieker & E. (H.) Carmen (Eds.), *The gender gap in psychotherapy* (p. 33). New York: Plenum Press.

Courtois, C. A. (1988). *Healing the incest wound: Adult survivors in therapy.* New York: W. W. Norton & Company.

Covington, S. S. (1982). *Sexual experience, dysfunction, and abuse: A comparative study of alcoholic and nonalcoholic women.* Unpublished doctoral dissertation, Union Graduate School.

Miller, N. S. (1991). Special problems of the alcohol and multiple-drug dependent: Clinical interactions and detoxification. In R. J. Francis, & S. I. Miller (Eds.), *Clinical textbook of addictive disorders* (pp. 194-218). New York: Guilford Press.

Russo, N. F. (Ed.). (1985). *A women's mental health agenda.* Washington, D.C.: American Psychological Association.

Another Strand of Our Diversity:
Some Thoughts from a Feminist Therapist with Severe Chronic Illness

Jessica M. Barshay

SUMMARY. This article represents the author's attempt to open the subjects of disability and accessibility-for-all in the women's community and specifically the feminist therapy community. It is a revised version of a presentation given at the May 1990 Advanced Feminist Therapy Institute Conference in Chicago.

The author's illnesses, CFIDS (Chronic Fatigue Immune Dysfunction Syndrome) and MCS/EI (Multiple Chemical Sensitivity/ Environmental Illness) are "women's illnesses," and, as such, are generally misunderstood and ignored. For this reason, the author describes in some detail her personal experiences, physical and emotional, of becoming and being severely chronically ill. She discusses shortcomings in the women's therapy community's response to disabled women and suggests some analysis of the phenomenon of what she calls the "active unwillingness to know."

This article was originally read as a paper at the May 1990 conference of the Advanced Feminist Therapy Institute (AFTI), a conference which I was unable to attend in person, due to severe

---

Jessica M. Barshay, ACSW, holds California licenses in Clinical Social Work and Marriage, Family and Child Counseling. She has been a feminist therapist in private practice in Berkeley, CA, since 1973.

Correspondence may be addressed to: Jessica M. Barshay, 2490 West Street, Berkeley, CA 94702.

[Haworth co-indexing entry note]: "Another Strand of Our Diversity: Some Thoughts from a Feminist Therapist with Severe Chronic Illness." Barshay, Jessica M. Co-published simultaneously in *Women & Therapy* (The Haworth Press, Inc.) Vol. 14, No. 3/4, 1993, pp. 159-169; and: *Women with Disabilities: Found Voices* (ed: Mary E. Willmuth, and Lillian Holcomb) The Haworth Press, Inc., 1993, pp. 159-169. Multiple copies of this article/chapter may be purchased from The Haworth Document Delivery Center [1-800-3-HAWORTH; 9:00 a.m. - 5:00 p.m. (EST)].

chronic illness. I would like to thank Marcia Hill for graciously, sight-unseen, agreeing to present the paper for me in my absence. As far as I know this mode of presentation was a first for AFTI, and as such in itself marked a move to include members who are too ill to attend conferences. I also wish to thank Jeanne Adleman for giving me the idea that I could present and that I had a worthwhile contribution to make as a member with severe chronic illness. My thanks go, too, to Else Bolotin and Kathleen Gates for accepting my proposal late and with this unusual mode of presentation. My deep gratitude goes to Esther Rothblum for taking it upon herself to edit my talk for publication and to submit it as my proposal to this volume. My greatest appreciation, however, is for my partner, Judith Masur, without whom I would have given up long ago in more areas than just writing.

As far as I know my talk at AFTI in 1990 was the first time that chronic illness had been addressed as a diversity issue in the feminist therapy community. It was also the first time that I "came out" in a public setting as a woman with severe chronic illness. Telling people that you are chronically ill is a risky affair, often devastating for reasons I will go into shortly. I have let people think many strange things about me rather than tell them I am ill; "Jessica is unfriendly," "Jess is a snob," "Jessica is not reliable," and so on. This article is significant for me because I intend to tell the truth about my situation.

Some disclaimers are in order. The twin subjects of disability and accessibility-for-all are large ones. They need to be raised by feminist therapists or by any organization that is committed to being inclusive of all our diversity as women. I want to make it clear that my goal in this article is simply to open the topics, using my own experience as a wedge or lever. I cannot speak for all women who are ill, nor even for all women with my own illness. Some of my experiences will probably generalize, and when I think they do I will point it out, but I make no claims to universality. We will need the voices of many disabled and ill women before we can know what needs to be done to include us all. This article is only a beginning.

The illness that hit me in October 1985 is now known in the U.S. as CFIDS (see-fids), an acronym for Chronic Fatigue Immune Dysfunction Syndrome. Some of you may know it by its former names: EBV (Epstein-Barr Virus), Chronic Mononucleosis or the demeaning "Yuppie Flu." In Canada it is generally now known as M.E. (Myalgic Encephalomyelitis), a name I like better because it sounds serious, mysterious and incapacitating, all of which CFIDS, by any name, is.

The basic facts about the syndrome are explained in a sheet entitled "A CFIDS Primer" and can be obtained from the CFIDS Association, Community Health Services, P. O. Box 220398, Charlotte, NC 28222, telephone (704) 362-CFID.

I will just mention a few things you need to know in order that the rest of this article makes sense to you. CFIDS is an extremely complex illness. As of this writing, May 1990, CFIDS is incurable although some symptoms can be alleviated by medication. The mode of transmission is unknown but it seems not to be easily contagious except perhaps in the early stages. There is good reason to believe its basic cause is a virus, quite probably a retrovirus, which is a rare kind that reproduces in some way that other viruses do not. I think the only other known human retrovirus is the HIV virus that causes AIDS. Unlike AIDS, however, CFIDS is not sexually transmitted, and also unlike AIDS, it is not a killer disease. In fact, some have termed CFIDS "the perfect virus" since it can prey on all body systems for an indefinite period of time, continually reproducing itself and never killing its victim. CFIDS has some features of an autoimmune disease like lupus or rheumatoid arthritis which involve a hyperimmunity where the body actually becomes allergic to its own secretions. Apparently because of the hyperimmunity, CFIDS patients do not present with opportunistic infections as do PWA's (People With AIDS). In many PWC's (as we affectionately call ourselves), especially those with a history of allergy, CFIDS can also cause severe environmental sensitivities, which is to say that one can become allergic to just about everything. One of the best articles on the subject of environmental allergy, which can also occur as a syndrome independent of CFIDS, was written in 1985 by AFTI's new administrator, Polly Taylor (Taylor, 1985).

The hallmark symptom of CFIDS is a crushing fatigue, malaise and weakness which does not resolve with any amount of rest. The remainder of the symptom picture is the bewildering array of disorders listed in the "CFIDS Primer." The configuration differs from individual to individual and is unstable even in the medical history of one individual, with symptoms coming and going in an unpredictable manner and varying from mild to severe. Some of you may be thinking that this illness sounds very strange, rather like a "symptom salad," and you may be wondering how it all comes together as a single disease. Indeed medical science has been baffled by the same considerations and questions, complicated by the fact that CFIDS is primarily a "women's disease," that CFIDS patients have abnormal reactions to medication, and that we are not a population that can be counted on to get well, or better, or to die. Even now, when a great deal is in fact known about the disease, most M.D.'s and psychiatrists remain ignorant of it or actually believe it doesn't exist. This is true in spite of the fact that in March, 1988, the Centers for Disease Control came out with specific criteria for CFIDS, thus allowing it to enter the lexicon of "real" diseases. CFIDS is as recognizable a medical entity as, say, Borderline Personality Syndrome is a psychological one–providing you know what patterns to look for.

For unknown reasons, CFIDS is primarily a women's disease. As of 1990 statistics seem to indicate that it strikes women three to four times more often than men. Personally I think that the ratio is actually much larger. Because women are poorer and have less access to medical care and coverage than men do, I believe many women never enter the data pool from which statistics are drawn. A great deal can be said and needs to be said about the state of women's health care in the U.S. and the politics and economics involved. These issues are beyond the scope of this paper, but they have been well addressed by Jackie Winnow (1989), founder of the Women's Cancer Resource Center, in her article entitled, "Is AIDS Draining the Women's Community?" Suffice it to say here that the particular form which medical misogyny takes in the case of CFIDS is to simply deny the existence of the illness. It is possible to do this in part because there is no laboratory test which confirms the presence of CFIDS, and in part because the diagnosis protocol involves extremely costly procedures to rule out all other possible diseases that resemble CFIDS in some features. Thus many women remain undiagnosed, misdiagnosed, untreated, mistreated, disbelieved or sent to psychiatrists as depressives or hysterics or somatoform hypochondriacs–and that is if they get any medical attention at all.

In my own case I was more fortunate than many. It was only two and one-half years after the onset of my illness that I found a fine woman M.D. who believed in CFIDS. I cannot entirely blame my HMO, Kaiser Health Plan, for the two and one-half years, although my doctors there certainly did not take my complaints seriously or attempt in any way to find out what was wrong with me. However, I knew several women with EBV, as it was called then, and my own dread, fear and denial delayed my diagnosis at least as much as the medical system did. I just did not want to have that awful illness.

Even after my diagnosis my condition continued to deteriorate for many months as the virus ran its initial and most virulent course. I spent three months in bed, barely able to reach for a glass of water on my bedside table. My life fell apart. My private practice went on hold. I will talk some later about the psychological effects of CFIDS, but during this acute period and for some time after I began to improve, I literally had no emotional life. I was just too sick for it. I learned that there is such a thing as being too sick to have feelings.

Very gradually, with the addition of one medicine after another tried, about two-thirds of them failing or producing bad side effects, some began to help me and I began to improve. I can almost hear the sigh of relief coming up from the reader, so I must hasten to explain what this improved state is like. My condition has been relatively stable for about a year, but it is a stability very far from the semblance of wellness, and I have no rational reason to expect further improvements. I have exhausted all the known medical possibilities and many alternative ones as well. At present I have between two and six useable hours per day, that is to say hours that I can spend not sleeping or resting. I have resumed a half-time practice of 10 to 12 client-hours per week. On a good day I can see three clients in my home office, take care of my bodily needs and occasionally do part of what I call my "triathlon," a walk around the block with my dogs, five minutes on my exercise bike and 10 minutes of Chinese stretching exercises. On a bad day I'm flat on my back all day, unable to read because of eye muscle weakness and the inability to hold a book and usually unable to tolerate light or sound. I have about half good and half bad days.

Aside from the constant exhaustion, I suffer from leg cramps, painful lymph glands in my neck and sore throat all the time, and a variety of other symptoms more or less debilitating, some old and some new, at different times. I am one of those with a history of allergy so I have developed severe environmental illness which makes it virtually impossible for me to go anywhere even if I should feel well enough to go out. Ten to 15 times a day I have some medical event or other, be it swallowing pills, giving myself a shot, taking a pile of vitamins, diluting powders in water to drink or snorting weird hormone drops up my nose. My timer goes off about once an hour to remind me of the next medicine; this is a standing joke in my house. I have 19 prescriptions which I must keep filled, about a dozen of which I take every day and the rest only as needed for particular symptoms.

My present state of health is bought at the cost of about $1,000 per month and adherence to a rigorous protocol of sleep, rest, diet, medication and avoidance of toxic exposures. It comes down to staying home with my air purifier on 90% of the time and feeling anywhere from sick to very, very sick 95% of the time anyway. Any increase in activity level or change in protocol has immediate negative consequences; my symptoms worsen or new ones appear.

The psychological reality of living in this terrible diminished world with no end in sight requires a paper of its own and that is one I hope to write one day. Briefly, I will say here that isolation is a very big problem, perhaps the biggest psycho-social consequence of CFIDS. Old friends have a hard time accepting my situation as it is now, and I have lost several important ones. I do not have the energy to make new friends or even to keep up with women I already know, for an extra telephone call in my day will often bring on an exacerbation of symptoms. I am constantly recycling the famous "stages of grief" in a way which I think is particular to severe chronic illness, for a state of acceptance is a different accomplishment under conditions of unpredictable symptoms in constant flux. I notice that narcissistic traits once relatively small in my character now loom large, especially self-referring and envy. Paranoia, although difficult to recognize when everything really *is* a danger, has made an unwelcome appearance in my personality. I am saved from bitterness and despair, most of the time anyway, by having a good sense of humor, a loving partner since 1981, two good friends with CFIDS, both therapists themselves, to talk to, and a long history of spiritual practice.

Social isolation, exclusion and invisibility are not intrinsic to the experience of illness. They are socially constructed. Why they should be is a very interesting question indeed. I have two quotes which shed some light on the subject. I owe them both to my dear friend Linda Zaretsky, a psychotherapist and political activist who has had severe CFIDS since 1976, yet retains one of the liveliest and most acute minds I have ever known. She and I have spent many a telephone talk pondering questions about CFIDS from many angles, and these two quotations are meaningful to both of us.

The first is from Primo Levi (1988), the Jewish-Italian writer of the Holocaust who committed suicide a few years ago. In the preface of his last book *The Drowned and The Saved,* he writes, ". . . this same thought ['even if we were to tell it, we would not be believed'] arose in the form of nocturnal dreams produced by the prisoners' despair. Almost all the survivors, orally or in their written memoirs, remember a dream which frequently recurred during the nights of imprisonment, varied in its detail but uniform in its substance: they had returned home and with passion and relief were describing their past sufferings, addressing themselves to a loved one, and were not believed, indeed were not even listened to" (p. 12).

The second is from Simone Weil's book *Waiting for God,* from an essay entitled "The Love of God and Affliction." This woman, a French Jewish intellectual turned Catholic after World War II, wrote in 1951, "Men [sic] have the same carnal nature as animals. If a hen is hurt, the others rush upon it, attacking it with their beaks. This phenomenon is as automatic as gravity. Our senses attach all the scorn, all the revulsion, all the hatred that our reason attaches to crime, to affliction. . . . everybody despises the afflicted, to some extent, although practically no one is conscious of it or will admit it" (p. 122).

It is my contention that these two factors, disbelief and hatred, so eloquently described for us by Levi and by Weil, account for much of the isolation, exclusion and invisibility experienced by women with CFIDS. We are prisoners, not of war but of a virus, and we are regularly, systematically and institutionally disbelieved. I do not know of any other serious illness in which the sufferer must struggle to get others to believe she has a disease.

I think the kind of hatred Weil seems to mean needs some further explication, lest it be too difficult for us to see in ourselves because it is so ego-dystonic. We do know, as psychotherapists, that just because something is unconscious and ego-dystonic does not mean it doesn't exist; in fact it is likely to exist in its most destructive form precisely to the extent that it is not recognized and accepted by the self. Many of you are familiar with D. W. Winnicott's well-known essay "Hate in the Countertransference," written in 1947. It has appeared in several collections of his work, one of them cited in my bibliography. He is speaking specifically of the hatred the psychoanalyst feels for his psychotic patient, but along the way, in his own warm and unique way, Winnicott touches upon a normative kind of hatred which he seems to consider just another human emotion. He views it as one end of the continuum of which the other end is love, and implies that it is necessary to be able to hate in order to love. For Winnicott, hate is no big deal, as long as we recognize it and, of course, as psychotherapists, contain it. I think that it is in this meaning of hatred that Weil's imagery of the hens can be most useful to us as we think about severe chronic illness. This kind of hatred is probably present in our interactions with women with any serious illness, not just CFIDS.

With the ideas of disbelief and hatred in place, I would like to discuss my illness in relation to feminist therapists' commitment to diversity. Specifically, I note three kinds of invisibility in operation which will need to be corrected before women with chronic illness can be fully accepted and included.

The first is the simple invisibility of my not being present at the AFTI conference. When I became ill and had to stop participating in my usual activities and organizations, no one contacted me to find out why I wasn't there any more. The same thing happens to many other women with CFIDS in respect to their activities and organizations. It seems we are systematically not approached or asked what would make our participation possible. I am not clear exactly what AFTI's responsibility ought to be toward members who "drop out" due to illness, but it does seem to me now that there ought to be some institutional (as opposed to the more haphazard personal) channel of communication. It seemed perfectly normal to me at the time that my absence be ignored, but then most forms of repression seem perfectly normal until that moment when it "clicks" that something is not right. I now see the lack of outreach to members who are ill as a function of unconscious hatred.

If I were able to attend conferences, or go anywhere else in public, a second kind of invisibility would come into play: the fact that my disability is hidden as opposed to visible. That makes it easy to ignore. While I certainly do not look like a healthy woman, I suppose I might just as well be tired, or shy, or bored or any number of other things besides severely ill. Sooner or later the dreaded question comes, "So how are you?" Usually I say, "Okay, and you?" for ordinary social purposes. On the rare occasions that I want to risk some genuine contact, I have to say something about CFIDS. The overwhelming likelihood when I do is that the response will be, "Gee, you don't look sick," if it is in person or, "Gee, you don't sound sick," if it is on the phone. I think it is easy to perceive the disbelief and the hatred in these remarks. I do not mean to say they are the only emotions involved in a given interaction. There may well be concern, curiosity, compassion, fear and other feelings, but the most likely emotions to be unconscious and therefore dangerous are disbelief and hatred. Meaningful interchange comes to a halt between us as a result.

It seems to me that there are few things a person can say that feel as threatening to others as she is sick and nothing can be done about it. Another contender, in my experience, is for a fat woman to tell someone she is quite happy with herself and has no intention of going on a diet. Our culture generally overvalues activity, fitness and certain kinds of beauty. I'm speculating here but maybe in a women's organization like AFTI which promotes the strong, brave, powerful and productive woman, the spectre of a seriously chronically ill woman may be even more disturbing than it is elsewhere. Over and over again I have experienced what I call the active unwillingness of women to know the reality of my situation. It is the rare individual who can resist suggestion, "Have you tried healing crystals (homeopathy, dance therapy, affirmations, the candida diet, etc.,

etc.)?" I interpret a woman's compulsion to make suggestions as revealing her terror of my helplessness and of the same thing happening to her, her intense wishes to deny my helplessness and the possibility of her own, and thus her active unwillingness to know.

It would be unfair, however, for me to project all the responsibility onto other people. There is a good deal of my not wanting to tell dovetailing nicely with others' not wanting to hear. Some of the reasons are obvious: I don't like being the bearer of bad news and I don't like being disbelieved and hated. Over and beyond these comes something I could not have anticipated. I feel a sense of shame and self-hatred about being sick, and it sometimes silences me, even when there might be a possibility of real communication. I believe this is probably true for most women with severe chronic illness. Some, I know, also feel guilt, which for whatever reason I do not experience. We try to "pass-for-well," sometimes in order to avoid the hatred and disbelief of others, sometimes to avoid our own shame and self-hatred. It is as irrational to be ashamed of being sick as to be ashamed of being raped or beaten, but there it is, that deep and ancient woman-shame in another form. It also reminds me of the shame and silence which surrounded my grandparents' life of poverty in Russia: the shame of the oppressed. So it is possible that you may ask how I am, and you may have recognized and put aside your disbelief and hatred, and I still won't be able to tell you right away because I'm too ashamed of myself and what my life has become. You need to know this if you want to know me.

The women's therapy community has done little to include women who are ill or disabled. Temporarily able-bodied readers of this article–for none of us is farther away than a germ or a slip from illness or disability–should consider what a proactive stance would be toward inclusion of women with disabilities in our communities, our organizations, our therapy practices and our lives.

REFERENCES

Levi, P. (1988). *The drowned and the saved.* NY: Simon & Schuster, Inc.
Taylor, P. (1985). This confused, dreadfully lonely place. In *Broomstick: A National Feminist Magazine By, For and About Women over 40*; 3543 18th Street, #3, San Francisco, CA 94110, U.S. Individual subscriptions, $15/year and $5 for sample. (Polly Taylor is AFTI's new administrator. She wrote this article

for the Allergies and Other Disabilities Double Issue of Broomstick, Volume 7, #3 and #4.)

Weil, S. (1951). The love of God and affliction. In *Waiting For God*. New York: Harper Colophon Books.

Winnicott, D. W. (1958). Hate in the countertransference. In *Through pediatrics to psychoanalysis*. London: Hogarth Press. (This article was written in 1947.)

Winnow, J. (1989). Lesbians working on AIDS–Assessing the impact on health care for women. *Outlook National Lesbian & Gay Quarterly, 5*, 10.

Environmental Illness/Multiple Chemical Sensitivities: Invisible Disabilities

Pamela Reed Gibson

SUMMARY. Recent attention has focused on a hidden disability usually referred to as Multiple Chemical Sensitivities (MCS), Environmental Illness (EI), or Ecologic Illness, and involving detrimental effects upon multiple bodily systems in response to exposures to chemicals in levels that have been "generally regarded as safe" (GRAS). This article will briefly describe MCS/EI as a disability, with emphasis on the impediments to a productive life for persons who experience this syndrome. Economic and psychological issues which are likely to be present as a *result* of being forced to face life with this hidden and unacknowledged problem are discussed. Political and disability issues are discussed, and examples are provided of women coping with the various aspects of this illness. Therapists who wish to be supportive to this population are offered suggestions for caregiving.

Environmental Illness, Multiple Chemical Sensitivities, Ecologic Illness, and Chemical Hypersensitivity Syndrome are names used to

Pamela Gibson holds a PhD in Clinical Psychology and is Assistant Professor of Psychology, and a psychotherapist with interests in women's issues.

Correspondence may be addressed to: Pamela Gibson, PhD, James Madison University, Department of Psychology, Johnston Hall, Harrisonburg, VA 22807.

Pamela Gibson would like to thank Bernice Lott and Pamela Deiter for their helpful comments on this paper.

[Haworth co-indexing entry note]: "Environmental Illness/Multiple Chemical Sensitivities: Invisible Disabilities." Gibson, Pamela Reed. Co-published simultaneously in *Women & Therapy* (The Haworth Press, Inc.) Vol. 14, No. 3/4, 1993, pp. 171-185; and: *Women with Disabilities: Found Voices* (ed: Mary E. Willmuth, and Lillian Holcomb) The Haworth Press, Inc., 1993, pp. 171-185. Multiple copies of this article/chapter may be purchased from The Haworth Document Delivery Center [1-800-3-HAWORTH; 9:00 a.m. - 5:00 p.m. (EST)].

171

describe states of ill health that are caused by exposures to substances normally present in the environment. Environmental Illness is taken to be the more general term, and describes a state of ill health in which harmful reactions can be brought on by exposures to foods, molds, pollens, and dusts, as well as chemicals. Multiple Chemical Sensitivities refers more specifically to illness caused by exposures to chemicals. There is disagreement among those who study this problem regarding which term should be used. Because the political and personal ramifications are similar regardless of how specific one's triggers for illness are, this article will use the terms Environmental Illness (EI) and Multiple Chemical Sensitivities (MCS) interchangeably.

This article will briefly describe EI/MCS as a disability/chronic illness, with emphasis on the impediments to a productive life for persons who experience this syndrome. Although it is common knowledge that allergy can be a nuisance and a moderate health risk, few persons realize that reactions to environmental triggers may become so debilitating that those afflicted must make drastic lifestyle changes in order to survive–sometimes to the point of living practically in isolation.

DEMOGRAPHICS AND DESCRIPTION

Regardless of which term is used, persons who suffer from this problem constitute a hidden population of disabled persons, the majority of whom appear to be women. Researchers have found that women constitute from 70% (Report of the Ad Hoc Committee on Environmental Hypersensitivity Disorders, 1985; Davidoff, 1992) to 81% (Rippere, 1983) of those identified with EI/MCS.

Very little medical, economic, or psychological help is currently available for this population. Symptoms can affect any bodily system, and may include headaches, nausea, fatigue, dizziness, confusion, muscle weakness, depression, anxiety and many other physical and emotional reactions (Bell, 1982; Davidoff, 1989; Lewith & Kenyon, 1985; Randolph & Moss, 1982; Rippere, 1983; Rogers, 1986, 1988, 1990). Without strict adherence to a modified safe lifestyle, the tendency of this condition is generally to deteriorate–that is for reactions to become both more severe and to begin to occur in response to a wider variety of substances (Randolph & Moss, 1982). In some cases, the woman's health becomes so compromised that she is isolated and housebound.

In addition to the better known substances such as molds, dusts, pollens and foods commonly known to cause reactions, chemicals that have been identified as triggering reactions in susceptible persons include petrochemicals (including gasoline, diesel, propane, and other combustibles), formaldehyde, paints, thinners, resins, pipe and tobacco smoke, perfumes, chemical household cleaners, pesticides, chemical treatments on new clothing, printed materials (because of the solvents), and many other substances (Randolph & Moss, 1982; Rogers, 1986, 1990). It is important to understand that reactions to chemicals in large part are more serious than those commonly understood as consequences of allergy (e.g., simple sinusitis), and include neurotoxic effects which can seriously impair functioning. One otherwise stable and capable woman becomes so ill after a gas exposure (meaning any nearness to a gas stove, forced-air gas heat, a welding torch, a propane burner, or auto exhaust) that she experiences the following symptoms within minutes, and for three days following: head pains, weakness, confusion, depression, and tearfulness. These are debilitating reactions with serious implications relating to quality of life. Women who suffer effects this serious must make lifestyle accommodations that rob them of social, economic, and personal opportunities. Others' disbelief and/or lack of knowledge about this health problem only adds to the distress of those who suffer.

The research arm of the National Academy of Sciences has estimated that about 15% of the population may be affected by environmental illness (Davidoff, 1989), yet little has been done by legislators, educators, industry or the medical establishment to address the needs of the persons affected by this health threat. Feminists have identified many cultural stressors that negatively impact on women's mental health, but because we have no paradigm for chemicals as variables that may affect mental health, psychologists have done almost no work in this area. Exceptions are Rebecca Bascom's (1989) review of the literature commissioned by the Maryland Department of the Environment, the work of Linda Lee Davidoff and colleagues (Davidoff, 1991, 1992; Nethercott, Davidoff, Curbow, &

Abbey, 1992; Ziem & Davidoff, 1992), and that of Nancy Fiedler and colleagues (Fiedler, Maccia, & Kipen, 1992).

Nicholas Ashford and Claudia Miller's Report to the New Jersey State Department of Health (1989) reviewed the evidence for adverse reactions to low levels of chemicals in the environment. Readers who need to be convinced may review Ashford and Miller. It seems clear that persons with EI/MCS are credible and deserving of respect. Therapists need to be educated regarding the experiences of clients with this condition, and about the types of support/advice likely to be helpful.

The psychosomatic paradigm has had a tremendous influence upon medicine, psychology, and new age philosophies. The typical view is that physical conditions can have emotional etiologies. However, the opposite can also occur, i.e., physical causes can effect mental and emotional changes (Ashurst, 1987). The field of toxicology is full of examples, such as the CNS depression effects of inhalation of gasoline and many other chemicals. Although Theron Randolph has been writing about the mental health effects of chemicals since the 1950s, Randolph has not been accorded any more credibility by conventional medicine and psychology than have clients with environmental illness.

RUINED LIVES

Economic Issues

The poorer women are, and the more stressed in other ways, the less chance they have of identifying this health problem if they have it. Even women with informational and economic resources are unlikely to find a diagnosis easily. One woman suffered from severe fatigue, depression, headaches, digestive disturbances and insomnia for seven years with no hint that her illness was caused by hypersensitivity to natural gas. She identified the problem only after finding and reading Randolph and Moss' (1982) book *An Alternative Approach to Allergies.* For seven years, physicians had offered her drugs, operations, x-rays, and a multitude of vitamins. A woman with less resources knows only that she becomes ill when she cleans her apartment (sensitivity to cleaning solutions). Since she lives on public assistance in an inner-city neighborhood, and has no car, she has no access to safer cleaning solutions, appropriate medical treatment, books or consultation. The only women with even a small chance of correctly identifying their problem are women with ample resources.

However, even women with resources including health insurance are unlikely to be able to muster these resources as aids to improving their health. Because conventional medicine does not recognize this illness, those who suffer from and those who work with MCS often face hostility from the health industry. Health insurance is unlikely to pay for diagnosis or treatment. Consequently, women with the disabling conditions and their loved ones are often financially depleted in attempting to cope with the illness. The Ontario Ministry of Health has estimated that the average medical expenses for a patient with MCS over an eight year period are about $15,000 (Davidoff, 1989).

Financial strain is compounded by required lifestyle changes. For example, women may find that they are unable to tolerate their homes because of the gas or oil heating systems, formaldehyde insulation, or any number of other contaminants. Of those who have homes and can afford it, some have chosen to alter their homes rather than move out of them, and consultees have reported that the costs for this can reach or even exceed $100,000.

All this may well have to be tackled at the same time that the woman is discovering that her job contributes to her chemical exposure. Her income is therefore threatened as well.

The Stresses of Avoidance

If women with MCS/EI are able to identify ways to feel better, these often involve avoiding places where they are likely to be exposed to the offending substances. Rippere (1983) found that avoidance was one of the three highest rated self-help strategies for sensitive persons (the other two were education and self-help groups). For example, persons who are extremely sensitive to petrochemicals cannot hail cabs, ride buses, enter restaurants (or perhaps any building with a gas stove or direct forced-air petrochemical heat), use public laundromats (gas dryers), pump their own gas, or use public restrooms in gas stations. These extreme restrictions are all necessary in order to avoid petrochemicals. Yet most persons with MCS suffer from sensitivities to a *number* of classes of substances, and the task of avoidance becomes almost impossible even with heroic measures. Avoidance may include giving up eating in restaurants to avoid unsafe foods, gas cooking or cigarette smoke; limiting or avoiding travel because of exposures on the highway and in hotel rooms to paints, pesticides, chemical cleaners, chemicals used on bedding, bathroom sprays, etc., and not visiting other people's homes. Just walking outside may not be safe, as a walk down a suburban street can involve exposure to lawn chemicals, diesel fuel, factory emissions, construction site chemicals, and a multitude of other inhalants. Many women with MCS are indeed housebound, and constitute an invisible population.

PSYCHOLOGICAL ISSUES
FOR THE CHEMICALLY SENSITIVE

Direct Reactions

Psychological effects as a result of environmental illness/chemical sensitivity occur at two levels. Primary effects involve direct neurotoxic/psychological consequences of exposures. The toxicology literature is replete with examples of neurological and other toxic consequences of high levels of exposures to chemicals. Yet for persons who are unusually sensitive, toxic effects occur at low levels of exposure–levels "generally recognized as safe" (GRAS)–and the effects are influenced heavily by individual differences (just as they are for alcohol intake, bee stings, and snake bites). Finn (1987/88) has reviewed evidence for CNS, immune and cardiovascular effects of organic solvent sensitivity. Dager, Holland, Cowley and Dunner (1987) discussed cases of panic disorder precipitated by exposure to organic solvents and concluded that "a recurring idiosyncratic exposure can occur due to an underlying mechanism or vulnerability indistinguishable from that which causes panic attacks" (1987, p. 1058). Therapists may observe effects mimicking depression, anxiety, and other psychiatric "disorders" which are actually environmentally triggered. These may appear as the result of intermittent exposures, or may be chronic, if the woman lives in an environment that is unsafe for her or works in a "sick building." For example, a gas-sensitive woman who lives with gas heat or cooking may exhibit chronic depression, headache, or irritability. Much work needs to be done to identify chemical effects that mimic psychologically-induced conditions if women are not to suffer from misdiagnosis and inappropriate treatment. Ashford and Miller (1989) specifically state that the hypothesis of environmentally-induced disease "should be ruled out *before* a patient is labeled with a psychiatric diagnosis" (p. viii). Ziem and Davidoff (1992) stated, "It is an axiom of medicine that, when investigating the origins of illness, physiologic causes must be ruled out before ascribing psychologic etiologies. This has simply not been done for illnesses associated with low-level chemical exposure" (p. 89).

Secondary Effects

Secondary effects of MCS/EI are psychological consequences of coping with a debilitating illness, and include the following:

Loss. Persons with environmental illness mourn for their lost health, job, mobility, ability to be effective in the world, lifestyle, and friends who often do not believe that the persons are made ill by what they claim makes them ill. Relationships may become seriously strained when friends must make adjustments. Persons with severe sensitivities are limited in where they can go to interact with other people. They may also have to limit what exposures occur in their homes and therefore may not be able to tolerate their guests smoking, or wearing perfume, cosmetics, chemically treated clothing, or recently dry-cleaned clothing. Limitations such as these are certain to impact personal relationships in negative ways.

Isolation. The physical isolation which results from being unable to tolerate many public environments, and the mental isolation that comes from having a disease which no one understands constitute considerable stressors. It is important to note that these stressors are impinging on persons who are already overloaded with physical stressors. Victim-blaming ideologies in our culture further insulate these persons from any possible support networks.

Fear. The person with environmental illness experiences fear in relation to both short- and long-term aspects of life. Even safe areas of the environment may unpredictably become unsafe at any time. A woman who is sensitive to pipe smoke may attend parties hoping that no one will smoke, but must be constantly vigilant and prepared to leave on a moment's notice if someone lights a pipe. The pipe smoker is free to enjoy the evening while she must retreat to a safe place to repair or endure any effects of exposure. In addition to the daily stresses of this unpredictability, the person with MCS/EI fears for the future. Research on the long-term course of this illness is scant, but women's life stories often involve progressive deterioration. The person fears for the loss of both physical and cerebral abilities.

Anger. Anger is a normal reaction to loss, misunderstanding, and harm from exposures, discrimination, and misdiagnosis.

Obsessive-compulsive behaviors. Avoidance of environmental triggers can result in behaviors which may resemble obsessive-compulsive behaviors to those who do not understand the importance or the difficulty of avoidance. The person with MCS is rarely able to let her guard down and relax. As one chemically sensitive consultee stated: "It makes an obsessive-compulsive out of you."

Self-blame. The woman with EI/MCS may wonder if there is something she did to cause her body to weaken and become ill. Paradigms that blame illness on emotions or assert that everyone gets what they deserve, or that we "create our own environments" only serve to encourage this.

Lack of choice about what emotions to show in public. Most of us have at least some choice about what emotions we show in public, but since sensitivity reactions may be cerebral, and may be triggered at any moment without warning, the woman with chemical sensitivities may not be able to avoid showing uncomfortable negative emotions in public places or in contexts where she is likely to be punished for them. Women are generally perceived as more emotional than men (Shields & MacDowell, 1987); are assessed in sex-stereotyped ways by therapists (Broverman, Broverman, Clarkson, Rosenkrantz, & Vogel, 1970; Fabrikant, 1974; Maslin & Davis, 1975); and are diagnosed by therapists as being histrionic more often than men are even if the symptomatology is identical (Hamilton, Rothbart, & Dawes, 1986), and even if the symptomatology corresponds to another DSM-III diagnosis (Ford & Widiger, 1989). Indeed, if Kaplan (1983) is right that the healthy woman in our culture automatically earns the diagnosis of histrionic, then women with MCS/EI are at a double disadvantage.

Lack of privacy about health. Persons with health problems which do not interfere with work may choose how much of their health information to make public, but for persons who often have to negotiate environmental changes in the workplace in order to be able to work at all, this privacy does not exist.

Loss of choice regarding a lifestyle that they will be comfortable with. MCS/EI often dictates so much about the outer conditions that are required in order to function, that little choice is left for the woman to make. One outgoing woman has been forced to endure isolation which does not suit her preference, or style, and thus is a source of even further stress. Having once worked with inner-city underserved populations, she must now be content to work in a carefully-chosen clean rural environment, if at all. In this way she is prevented from making a professional contribution where it is needed most.

Negative attitudes toward authorities/conventional medicine. Women with MCS/EI have had to self-educate and advocate in order to survive. Fiedler et al. (p.537, 1992) have discussed the distress experienced by MCS patients, citing "lack of understanding and acceptance by the medical practitioners they encounter." Because they have often received little or no help, or even ostracism and maltreatment from conventional medical practitioners, they naturally may expect helpers to misunderstand them and/or be inept at caregiving. Hence these clients may appear angry, "oppositional," "hysterical," or "paranoid" to potential helpers who do not understand their history of receiving inadequate medical and psychological care (P. J. Deiter, personal communication, April 3, 1992).

Classical conditioning. Many environments that were formerly a source of enjoyment may come to elicit negative associations for the person as they are paired with illness on a regular basis. A shopping trip which formerly felt like a day off may come to require constant vigilance and extreme care if the person is not to become ill.

Attributions are confusing. The person with EI may become anxious/depressed as a result of a chemical or other exposure, but may not be aware of what the exposure was. Consequently, she searches for the cause. Because our culture deals us no shortage of stressors, she may blame the upset on a psychological stressor which, although present, did not cause the reaction. The person is thus co-opted into mistakenly questioning her own psychological coping ability.

All resources are taken up with coping with the illness. For a person with severe MCS/EI, just surviving takes up so much time and energy that all other personal/spiritual/intellectual growth gets put on hold. The person "treads water," while mourning for the loss of her aspirations. As one former school psychologist said "This disease has taken away my motivation to work."

The loss of a continued stable sense of identity. In his book on chronic illness, Anselm Strauss (1984) has discussed the loss of a continuous sense of identity that occurs for the person who is chronically ill. In any form of chronic illness, the person's sense of self and well-being may fluctuate depending upon her current physical state. Since the exposures in MCS often cause emotional reactions that feel so different from the person's usual state of mind, there may come to be a discontinuous feeling of identity. When not reacting, the person cannot imagine being that sick. While reacting, previous experiences of feeling well, and previously established growth and direction, cannot be accessed. Therefore, identity comes to be punctuated by periods of limbo, during which the person suffers and waits for exposure effects to wear off.

Because of this the process of accepting illness is also interrupted. The process of acceptance with MCS/EI is interrupted by periods of feeling good during which the person begins as much as possible to push the illness out of consciousness. The next exposure is thus a devastating experience as the person was hoping that the disease, which had not reared its head for a while, was gone.

WHAT CLINICIANS SHOULD KNOW

Client Credibility

Therapists should know that not everyone writing in this area is sympathetic to the client's viewpoint, and that the client's self-esteem is likely to suffer in a culture which does not afford her illness legitimacy. The experience of lesbians/gays and others who have historically been socially ostracized are similar to the experience of women with MCS. Researchers have attempted to show psychological origins of EI/MCS much as they once attempted to identify lesbians and gays as psychologically unbalanced. Indeed, our culture has offered no shortage of "scientific" opinions regarding the behaviors of many oppressed groups. Landrine (1988) has cited a variety of examples of prominent men's views of oppressed populations. Slaves who ran away were said by Samuel Cartwright to suffer from a psychopathology ostentatiously titled "drapetomania." Women who have been chemically damaged are no different from other oppressed groups when it comes to having their complaints demeaned or trivialized. Persons who report experiencing symptoms as a result of environmental exposures have been diagnosed as having somatoform disorder (Brodsky, 1983) and have been said to need "deprogramming" of beliefs that chemicals are making them sick (ADA regulations on MCS, The Delicate Balance, IV, 3-4, 1991). If clients heed such advice, they are likely to exacerbate their symptoms, and reduce their chances of identifying and recovering from the problem. Although avoidance responses may appear obsessive to those unfamiliar with MCS, Davidoff (1992) has referred to these responses as "therapeutic and adaptive," as they can be helpful in avoiding reactions.

There is no evidence that EI/MCS is psychologically caused. Preliminary work by Linda Davidoff and her colleagues at the Johns Hopkins University School of Public Health and Hygiene does not support the hypotheses that MCS is psychologically caused, or that patients with MCS are characterized by persisting negative affect (Davidoff, 1991).

Political/Environmental Aspects

Therapists must recognize that we live in a world where new chemicals are synthesized every second. No longer do our immune systems have hundreds of years between inventions in which to adapt to new types of exposures. Many environmental critics believe that persons with chemical sensitivities are like the "canaries down the mineshaft," demonstrating what will come to pass for many persons as our chemical exposure continues to take its toll. This is the position of Ralph Nader's Public Citizen's group.

Clients will need support in dealing with often hostile health and legal systems. At a time when some researchers are beginning to investigate the effects of chemical exposures, chemical companies have much to gain by discrediting the person with environmental illness.

THE IMPORTANCE OF THERAPIST EDUCATION

Therapists should have a basic knowledge of this illness, and be aware that not all psychological symptoms are psychologically caused. Randolph and Moss (1982) present an excellent discussion of adaptation to chemicals in the early phases of the illness, and then draw parallels to addictive conditions such as alcohol use. Without an understanding that initial exposures may actually cause excitatory/hypomanic effects which later disappear as the person's system becomes depleted, therapists may not recognize the early phase of this illness. Therapists should study Randolph's chapter on adaptation cycles in order to learn to recognize various stages of this syndrome. For example, as the individual adapts to constant low-level exposures of the offending substance, the symptoms may become *masked* and thus unable to be deciphered without a period out of the offending environment. Upon re-exposure, symptoms will appear in a more pronounced and clear manner, allowing for accurate diagnosis (Ashford & Miller, 1989; Randolph & Moss, 1982).

Although writers like Brodsky (1983) have suggested advising clients against avoiding substances that the clients believe make them sick, we are ethically bound not to give advice that is likely to harm clients further. Just as therapists are bound not to deviate from areas of expertise regarding other problems, there are professional liability issues involved in giving advice that can later be shown to have been harmful. Mary Lamielle, President of the National Center for Environmental Health Strategies (NCEHS), in discussing work-place exposures in particular, has warned that "Those experiencing more severe symptoms require immediate removal from triggering exposures to minimize reactions and to avert permanent disability" (Indoor Air Quality Update).

Therapists need to know that clients with EI/MCS are likely to have "multiple symptoms involving multiple organ systems" (Ashford & Miller, 1989). These symptoms may sound subjective, and may not be easily diagnosable by tests which rely on end-organ damage for diagnosis. One does not have to exhibit a brain tumor in order to suffer from disabling headaches.

Therapists should question clients regarding recent environmental changes or exposures like home redecorating, installation of carpet, use of pesticides, or other situations which may be temporally related to the appearance of symptoms. Ashford and Miller (1989) point out that there are two types of exposure which may "initiate hypersusceptibility"–large overwhelming exposures and low-level repeated exposures. An example of a large exposure is an incident that occurred at the Environmental Protection Agency. New carpet installed in the EPA headquarters was the recent trigger for a number of EPA employees to become ill, and some have become permanently chemically sensitive as a result of their exposure to the 4-Phenylcyclohexane (4-PC) used in backing the carpet (Hirzy & Morison, 1989).

DISABILITY ISSUES

Optimistic news in regard to the allocation of resources for this disability is that the condition is recognized by the US Department of Housing and Urban Development (HUD) and the Social Security Administration (SSA) (Davis, 1991), and that some persons with EI/MCS are included in the Americans with Disabilities Act of 1990 (ADA). In interpreting ADA, The Justice Department has stated, in reference to environmental sensitivities, that:

> Sometimes respiratory or neurological functioning is so severely affected that an individual will satisfy the requirements to be considered disabled under the regulation. Such an individual would be entitled to all of the protections afforded by the Act. ("Excerpts from ADA regulations," 1991, p. 20-21)

Several persons with MCS were invited and attended the signing of ADA. But the majority of those who experience this syndrome have yet to receive the intended protection that disability status would afford them. EI/MCS is not totally accepted by the disability community. Because these individuals are not often recognized by appearance (that is, the disability is invisible), they are unlikely to encounter much sympathy from others. A therapist who offers her client acceptance and credibility goes a long way toward mitigating the negative effects of societal disbelief in the client's condition.

REFERENCES

ADA regulations on MCS. (1991). *The delicate balance*, Vol. 4, Nos. (3-4), p.14. Available from The National Center for Environmental Health Strategies, 1100 Rural Avenue, Voorhees, NJ 08043.

Ashford, N.A., & Miller, C.S. (1989). *Chemical sensitivity: A report to the New Jersey State Department of Health.*

Ashurst, P. M. (1987). Matter over mind: Psychosomatic or somatopsychic? *Clinical Ecology, 5*,(2), 75-80.

Bascom, R. (1989). *Chemical hypersensitivity syndrome study.* Prepared at the request of the State of Maryland Department of the Environment in response to 1988 Maryland Senate Joint Resolution 32.

Bell, I. R. (1982). *Clinical Ecology: A new medical approach to environmental illness.* Bolinas, CA: Common Knowledge Press.

Brodsky, C. M. (1983). Psychological factors contributing to somatoform diseases attributed to the workplace. *Journal of Occupational Medicine, 25*, 459-464.

Broverman, I. K., Broverman, D. M., Clarkson, F. E., Rosenkrantz, P. S., & Vogel, S. R. (1970). Sex-role stereotyping and clinical judgements of mental health. *Journal of Consulting and Clinical Psychology, 34*, 1-7.

Dager, S.R., Holland, J.P., Cowley, D.S., & Dunner, D.L. (1987). Panic disorder precipitated by exposure to organic solvents in the work place. *American Journal of Psychiatry, 144*, 1056-1058.

Davidoff, L. L. (1989, Winter). Multiple chemical sensitivities. *The Amicus Journal*, 13-23.

Davidoff, L.L. (1991, November). *Multiple chemical sensitivities: Research on psychiatric/psychosocial issues.* Paper presented at the symposium Multiple Chemical Sensitivity and the Environment II: Diagnosis and Therapy at the Annual meeting of the American Public Health Association, Atlanta, GA.

Davidoff, L.L. (1992). Models of multiple chemical sensitivities (MCS) syndrome: Using empirical data (especially interview data) to focus investigations. *International Journal of Toxicology and Industrial Health, 8*, 229-247.

Davis, E. (1991, December). Panel discussion; Responding to chemical sensitivity in the workplace. *Indoor Air Quality Update*, 5-6.

Fabrikant, B. (1974). The psychotherapist and the female patient. In V. Franks & V. Burtle (Eds.). *Women in Therapy.* New York: Brunners/Mazel.

Fiedler, N., Maccia, C., & Kipen, H. (1992). Evaluation of chemically sensitive patients. *Journal of Occupational Medicine, 34*, 529-538.

Finn, R. (1987/88). A review: Organic solvent sensitivity. *Clinical Ecology, 5*, 155-158.

Ford, M.R., & Widiger, T.A. (1989). Sex bias in the diagnosis of histrionic and antisocial personality disorders. *Journal of Consulting and Clinical Psychology, 57*, 301-305.

Hamilton, S., Rothbart, M., & Dawes, R. M. (1986). Sex-bias, diagnosis and DSM-III. *Sex Roles, 15*, 269-274.

Hirzy, J.W., & Morison, R. (1989, Oct.). *4-Phencyclohexane/carpet toxicity: The EPA headquarters case*. Paper presented at the Annual Meeting of the Society for Risk Analysis. San Francisco.

Kaplan, M. (1983). A woman's view of DSM-III. *American Psychologist, 38*, 786-792.

Indoor Air Quality Update (1991, December). p. 5. Cuttler Information Corp., Lamielle, M. (1991, December). Panel discussion: Responding to chemical sensitivity in the workplace. *Indoor Air Quality Update* pp. 6-7. Cuttler Information Corp.

Landrine, H. (1988). Revising the framework of abnormal psychology. In P. Bronstein & K. Quina (Eds.), *Teaching a psychology of people: Resources for gender and sociocultural awareness*. (pp. 37-44). American Psychological Association.

Lewith, G.T. & Kenyon, J.N. (1985). *Clinical ecology: The treatment of ill-health caused by environmental factors*. Wellingborough, Northamptonshire: Thorsons Publishers Limited.

Maslin, A., & Davis, J.L. (1975). Sex-role stereotyping as a factor in mental health standards among counselors-in-training. *Journal of Counseling Psychology, 22*, 87-91.

Nethercott, J.R., Davidoff, L.L., Curbow, B., & Abbey, H. (1992). Multiple chemical sensitivities syndrome: Toward a working case definition. Manuscript submitted for publication.

Randolph, T. G., & Moss, R. W. (1982). *An alternative approach to allergies*. New York, NY: Harper & Row.

Report of the Ad Hoc Committee on Environmental Hypersensitivity Disorders. (1985, Aug 17) Ontario Ministry of Health, Canada. (Available from Honorable Murray J. Elston, Minister of Health, 10th Floor, Hepburn Block, Toronto, Ontario, Canada M7A2C4.)

Rippere, V. (1983). *The allergy problem: Why people suffer and what should be done*. Wellingborough, Northamptonshire: Thorsons Publishers Limited.

Rogers, S. A. (1986). *The EI syndrome*. Syracuse, NY: Prestige Publishers.

Rogers, S. A. (1988). *You are what you ate*. Syracuse, NY: Prestige Publishers.

Rogers, S. A. (1990). *Tired or toxic?* Syracuse, NY: Prestige Publishers.

Shields, S. A. & MacDowell, K.A. (1987). "Appropriate" emotion in politics: Judgments of a televised debate. *Journal of Communication*, 78-89.

Strauss, A.L. (1984). *Chronic illness and the quality of life*. St. Louis, MO: C.V. Mosby Company.

Ziem, G. E., & Davidoff, L.L. (1992). Illness from chemical "odors": Is the health significance understood? Editorial. *Archives of Environmental Health, 47*, 88-91.

Disability in Female Immigrants with Ritually Inflicted Genital Mutilation

Hanny Lightfoot-Klein

SUMMARY. There have been 200,000 immigrants to the United States from African and Arab countries in the past decade that practice extensively disabling ritual genital mutilation. Many of these women are severely disabled not only by the social constraints placed upon them by their culture, but by chronic pain syndrome and mobility impairment. They only rarely present at conventional medical facilities, being prevented from doing so by protective/dominant men, and further by the fact that they have little or no expectation that their specialized medical problems will be either understood or dealt with compassionately. The disabling immediate and long term medical consequences of female genital mutilation are described, most particularly in relation to menstruation and childbirth. Its significance as a social phenomenon is explained in historical terms and in terms of the values of the societies in which it is tenaciously entrenched. The question of how a working relationship with these immigrant women may be established is discussed.

Between 1979 and 1984, Hanny Lightfoot-Klein spent a total of 32 months of concentrated, solitary, unfunded and self-motivated field research in Sudan, Kenya and Egypt, researching the topic of female genital mutilation. The area of her most intensive research was northern and central Sudan, where the practices are particularly severe and ubiquitous. She gained access to medical installations of all sorts, lived with Sudanese families, in the capital, in towns, villages and desert oases, and witnessed numerous births.

Correspondence may be addressed to: Hanny Lightfoot-Klein, 7300 N. Mona Lisa Road, Apt. 8245, Tucson, AZ 85741.

[Haworth co-indexing entry note]: "Disability in Female Immigrants with Ritually Inflicted Genital Mutilation." Lightfoot-Klein, Hanny. Co-published simultaneously in *Women & Therapy* (The Haworth Press, Inc.) Vol. 14, No. 3/4, 1993, pp. 187-194; and: *Women with Disabilities: Found Voices* (ed: Mary E. Willmuth, and Lillian Holcomb) The Haworth Press, Inc., 1993, pp. 187-194. Multiple copies of this article/chapter may be purchased from The Haworth Document Delivery Center [1-800-3-HAWORTH; 9:00 a.m. - 5:00 p.m. (EST)].

187

Selva is readying herself for admission to University Hospital, where she will give birth to her third child. She has two other children, both born in El Obeid, a remote town in the interior of Sudan. Within recent years, the family has migrated to the United States, where Selva's husband is presently a graduate student at the university.

Some of Selva's compatriots, who are also presently living under similar circumstances, help her pack the small suitcase that she will take with her. Saffia, who has already given birth in a U.S. hospital, elicits a general outburst of laughter when she impishly advises Selva: "Don't forget to tell them all about your automobile accident!"

To the uninitiated outsider, it is sometimes difficult to understand what causes such ready laughter among the oppressed, the mutilated and the disabled. Saffia's admonition to Selva is obviously a familiar, well worn "inside joke," one that is understood by all the other women in the room. The laughter in response to Saffia's mocking advice is fuelled by the absurdity and frustration inherent in a kind of experience that all these women share. The medical establishment that they must deal with can at best be expected to be ignorant of and inadequate to their special needs, and at worst insensitive to them.

The fact that these women have had any dealings with the United States medical establishment at all, is in itself unusual (Shaw, 1985). It can be explained only by the fact that their husbands or other protecting male family members accompanying them are highly educated, and relatively Westernized. Unless this special situation is the case, sexually mutilated immigrant women are only rarely seen by American doctors or nurses.

There have been an estimated 200,000 immigrants into the United States in the past decade from countries where female genital mutilation is customary. The women among them constitute a practically invisible and certainly silent entity where U.S. medical services are concerned (Garp, 1990).

Primary among the reasons for this is the fact that in order to obtain medical treatment, women from such cultures must first obtain the permission of their husbands or other dominant/protective male relatives. The woman can then only be examined or treated in his presence. In most cases, obtaining such permission is virtually impossible, unless all medical personnel involved is female. In many of the cultures from which these women originate, a woman is considered to have been dishonored if a man other than her husband touches her body.

Selva has not been in a car accident or any other accident. However, if the examining nurse or doctor has had no previous exposure to or understanding of her special condition, as is most likely to be the case, it is practically a certainty that she will be asked: "What happened to you? Were you in a car accident?" While such a question may give cause for mirth when the mutilated woman is among her peers, within a medical setting it elicits a justifiable anxiety in the patient that the health care practitioner will not know how to deal with her unique problems (Lightfoot-Klein & Shaw, 1991).

Selva's genital area is perfectly smooth, devoid of all features save a median scar running from the mons veneris down to a considerably reduced vaginal aperture. Her condition is the result of ritual genital mutilation, to which she has been subjected in early childhood, as have been all the other girls in her family, village or tribe.

Ritual genital mutilation of females is still widely practiced, not only among tribes living in remote areas of Africa, as has been commonly believed in the Western World, but also in the cities, at all levels of society, in a greater part of the continent. Presently, it affects an estimated 100 million women in more than 25 countries of Africa. It is also found to exist, albeit far more sporadically, in regions along the Arab peninsula and occasionally in parts of Asia (Lightfoot-Klein, 1989a).

In regions where the least drastic mutilations are customary, girls are made to suffer "only" partial clitoridectomy. In other regions, the entire clitoris and/or inner labia may be excised. Along the Horn of Africa, however, in an easterly area encompassing Southern Egypt, Northern and Central Sudan, parts of Ethiopia, Kenya, Somalia and Djibouti, and also Mali in West Africa, a far more extensive and devastatingly damaging procedure is the norm.

This procedure, known as Pharaonic Circumcision, consists of the excision of the clitoris, the inner labia and all but the skin of the outer labia. This remaining skin is then stitched up over the wound, in such a way that only a tiny opening remains, one which ideally does not exceed the width of a matchstick. The resulting bridge of skin and fibrous scar tissue is known as "infibulation." It serves, in effect, as the ultimate chastity belt, in societies where premarital chastity of women is of paramount importance. Intactness of the infibulation at marriage is testimony to the virginity of the bride, and thereby the honor of her family (Saadawi, 1980).

When a girl has been infibulated, she must urinate thereafter by slowly squeezing out her urine drop by painful drop. Disabling infections are a common consequence, as progressively more urinary debris accumulates behind the blockage, infections that may ultimately spread throughout the entire reproductive and renal systems (Dareer, 1982; Koso-Thomas, 1987; Verzin, 1975). This problem is compounded yet further when the girl matures sexually and begins to menstruate. It is virtually impossible for a tightly infibulated virgin to express her menstrual blood. Much of it may eventually clot behind the infibulation and simply remain there. A normal 3-5 day menstrual period stretches on into as many as 10 days, while the girl is often so disabled by pain and toxicity, that she is unable to attend school or hold a job (Lightfoot-Klein, 1989a, 1989c).

To escape this monthly agony, the infibulated young woman now finds herself between a rock and a hard place. It is to her advantage to have her family arrange for her marriage as soon as is possible after menstruation ensues, for when she marries, the infibulation that blocks menstrual discharge will be partially torn or cut open, in order to make sexual intercourse possible. This procedure may be done by the husband, by a relative of the husband or by a midwife. Whichever is the case, it inescapably subjects the bride to yet more trauma and pain, for her husband must then gradually enlarge the wound and prevent it from healing shut once more. This process may take agonizing weeks and even months to accomplish (Lightfoot-Klein, 1989a).

The tragic saga of chronic pain and disability that is the lot of genitally mutilated women continues as she bears her children. The normal birth passage is blocked by the inelastic scar tissue of the infibulation, endangering the lives of both mother and infant. It must be cut open to allow birth to take place, and is stitched up again later, usually once more to a matchstick sized opening, which the husband then has to once more widen, again with great pain to the woman.

All of these invasive and disabling procedures, which are "women's business" are generally arranged for by women elders (the grandmothers) and most usually executed by midwives, who hold considerable power over the lives of women and thereby occupy a highly respected position in the community (Lightfoot-Klein, 1989a).

Because women who have been sexually mutilated have grown up in cultures where female circumcision (as it is euphemistically called) is a matter of course, they regard it as altogether normal and are persuaded that it is absolutely necessary to their health and social acceptability. A girl who has not been circumcised is considered to be unclean, unmarriageable, and deserving only of pity (Lightfoot-Klein, 1989b).

It may come as a shock to Western women who first enter into contact with these practices and their consequences, that even *educated* women within the cultures that perform them may be among their staunchest advocates. This phenomenon becomes more comprehensible once it is understood that *un*circumcised women have been historically associated with slaves, prostitutes and other non-male-protected women of low caste, whose even sadder lot in life has always made them, and even more poignantly, their children, easy prey to rapists, marauders and slavers (Lerner, 1986).

If some of us should still find the evident barbarity of these customs incomprehensible, we might turn our attention to the fact that in the male-dominated United States medical establishment total extirpation of the female reproductive system is still the treatment of choice, even for non-life-threatening conditions. We might also note that 58% of our male newborns are subjected to routine, non-religious, medically unnecessary, unquestionably painful, generally unanesthetized circumcisions. The rationale for this invasive procedure is based on such flimsy scientific evidence that no other country in the Western World any longer accepts it (Wallerstein, 1980).

Most female genital mutilations are also still carried out without any anesthesia, under the most horrendously septic conditions. To those who survive them, they become a badge of honor, a source of pride. In societies that seem to uniformly abhor the female sex organs as dangerous, ugly, disgusting and malodorous (Lightfoot-Klein, 1989a), having these organs razed off becomes a rite of purification that ultimately leaves the girl feeling cleansed and beautified. When circumcised women are interviewed within the setting of their own culture in Africa and are asked, for example, how old they were when they were subjected to the rites, they are apt to say: "My family did this for me when I was (such and such an age)" (Lightfoot-Klein, 1989b). *For* me, not *to* me. A Sudanese survey reveals that 83% of Sudanese women strongly favor the practices, a figure that is barely distinguishable from the 87% obtained for men (Dareer, 1982).

When the health problems inherent in female genital mutilation are viewed from the outside by American disability culture, it becomes clearly apparent that genitally mutilated women suffer from multiple disabilities. They are victims of chronic pain syndrome, they manifest mobility impairment when they are so tightly sewn that their walk is reduced to a painful shuffle, they are missing an entire body part, they can not freely seek or obtain medical services without the permission and presence of a dominant male family member, in a system that generally has no understanding of or provisions for their special problem (Shaw, 1985).

When a genitally mutilated woman is living in her own country, where every other woman suffers much as she does, she accepts her disabilities as being "a woman's lot." When she is exposed to a Western culture, where what has been done to her is considered as being so bizarre that she quickly learns to live with it in silence, her disabilities may be compounded still further by emotional conflict and psychic pain.

As her awareness grows, she may understand for the first time that there is a connection between the procedure she has been subjected to in childhood, and the never ending, disabling episodes of pain that she yet suffers in consequence. She may begin to realize that she has been robbed of what is actually a valuable part of her body, the possession of which is not even questioned by women in her new environment. Quite possibly there may be a profound shift in the way she perceives herself and the society which has created her affliction. Because she is so lacking in power, this new perception will only serve to heighten her suffering.

How can we help such women? This is by no means a simple question to answer. To even begin such a process in our own country, we must first confront the powerful American taboo on sexual issues, by raising consciousness that a growing number of female immigrants to our shores are thus afflicted. Ideally, we would make health care services available to them, staffed exclusively by women, and at least in part by women who are native to their own part of the world. In order to be successful, such health care services would need to make provisions for involvement of the husbands, so as to gain their cooperation.

Beyond this, certain moral and ethical considerations will not be easy to resolve. Where do our most urgent obligations lie? With the victims of these damaging practices, or with their as yet intact daughters? Should we concern ourselves with creating and enacting laws that will deter immigrant peoples from mutilating their daughters within our own shores, so that they will not engender yet another generation of women who suffer from ritually inflicted disabilities? Do we have the right to interfere in this fashion with these peoples' centuries' old way of life? Would such a course of action not make us guilty once again of exactly the kind of racism and ethnocentrism that we are struggling to purge from our own society?

By some definitions, perhaps it would. Yet here, in the Decade of the Child, how can we passively condone the inevitable growth of an underground health care system of immigrant midwives, and thus allow them to carry on their lucrative trade in child mutilation unopposed? And is the execution of a health destroying, antiquated custom that is performed to make the girl *marriageable* meaningful in this country, where a variety of options other than marriage are open to her and continue to become open to her? Several European countries have already enacted laws that forbid the willful mutilation of children. In others, they are presently being debated.

Legislation forbidding the genital mutilation of girls has been on the books in a number of African countries for some decades, yet the practice has not yielded nor even abated as a result. All the same, such laws are not without potential merit, when, for example, educated African parents have become persuaded that their daughters should be allowed to remain intact, and they are opposed in this decision, as is often the case, by the elders of their family. Such parents may then make it clear to their family members that if their daughters are mutilated in their absence and against their will, (as has been the case in several instances), they will prosecute the perpetrators. The small beginnings of a movement to abolish these practices is already under way among African intellectuals. Although there is as yet little evidence of actual change, it may well be imminent. Within our own borders, we must actively encourage and support it.

REFERENCES

Dareer, A. (1982). *Woman, why do you weep?* London: Zed Press Ltd.

Garp, M. (1990). Unchosen chastity: African immigrants bring female circumcision to the U.S. *In These Times, 14* (32), 11-13.

Koso-Thomas, O. (1987). *The circumcision of women: A strategy for eradication.* London: Zed Press Ltd.

Lerner, G. (1986). *The creation of patriarchy.* New York: Oxford University Press.

Lightfoot-Klein, H. (1989 a). *Prisoners of ritual: An odyssey into female genital and circumcision in Africa.* New York: The Haworth Press, Inc.

Lightfoot-Klein, H. (1989 b). Rites of purification and their effects: Some psychological aspects of female genital circumcision and infibulation in an Afro-Arab Islamic society. *Journal of Psychology & Human Sexuality, 2* (2), 79-91.

Lightfoot-Klein, H. (1989 c). Ueber radikale Beschneidung von Frauen im Sudan (Radical Genital Mutilation of Women in Sudan). *Zeitschrift für Sexualforschung. 2* (2), 148-159.

Lightfoot-Klein, H., & Shaw, E. (1991). Special needs of ritually circumcised women patients. *Journal of Obstetrics, Gynecology and Neo-Natal Nursing, 20* (2), 102-107.

Saadawi, N. (1980). The hidden faces of Eve: Women in the Arab world. London: Zed Press.

Shaw, E. (1985). Female circumcision: Perception of clients and caregivers. *Journal of American College Health, 33* (5), 193-197.

Shaw, E. (1985). Female circumcision: What kind of maternity care do circumcised women need and can United States caregivers provide it? *American Journal of Nursing, 85*, 684-687.

Verzin, J. A. (1975). Sequelae of female circumcision. Tropical doctor, *5*, 163-169.

Wallerstein, E. (1980). *Circumcision: An American health fallacy.* New York: Springer Publishing Co.

Found Voices:
Women, Disability and Cultural Transformation

Deborah Lisi

SUMMARY. This article explores the cultural consequences of disability on women. The author interviewed four women with disabilities and two mothers and shares some of her own experiences with disability. The relationship between disability rights and feminism and ethnic identity and the impact of disability on the sense of self and personal goals are considered, as is the transformative power of speaking to the larger culture about how disability experiences inform human perceptions and social practices.

Women's entrance into the disciplines brings a recovery of voice and with it the realization that if we do not end a tradition of storm and shipwreck, there may well be an end to nature and to civilization. But women's questions also stir up conflict and disagreement and thus are more likely to be spo-

---

Deborah Lisi is a disability rights activist and policy consultant on disability issues in health care, education, arts programs, and human services. She works part time as the Executive Director for Vermont Protection and Advocacy, Inc., an organization which funds lay and legal advocacy for persons labeled mentally ill and developmentally delayed.

Correspondence may be addressed to: Deborah Lisi, R.R. 1, Box 1436, Waterbury, VT 05676.

[Haworth co-indexing entry note]: "Found Voices: Women, Disability and Cultural Transformation." Lisi, Deborah. Co-published simultaneously in *Women & Therapy* (The Haworth Press, Inc.) Vol. 14, No. 3/4, 1993, pp. 195-209; and: *Women with Disabilities: Found Voices* (ed: Mary E. Willmuth, and Lillian Holcomb) The Haworth Press, Inc., 1993, pp. 195-209. Multiple copies of this article/chapter may be purchased from The Haworth Document Delivery Center [1-800-3-HAWORTH; 9:00 a.m. - 5:00 p.m. (EST)].

195

> *ken where no one will leave and someone will listen. (Gilligan, 1990, p. 27)*

When individuals from a minority experience or culture enter the academic arena, they bring with them the voices of others of their kind, people whose life styles and personal connections have not led to the disciplines. It is not enough for these women and men to sit at the font of knowledge; they must enrich the substance of academia by adding to it the essence of the minority culture that has been left out of the thinking and debates of the universities and colleges. I believe in the value of those hidden and dishonored voices to strengthen, renew, and bring verity to our places of scholarship. So, I chose to interview women I know who deal with disability, not to write in the voice of the disciplines and scholarship but to honor what their experiences tell us about both the recovery of voice and the emergence of new voices among us.

Like the robin I saw outside my window this morning, red breasted in April snow, the voices of trailblazers carry spring seeds into a culture requiring change and renewal. The renewal of culture requires risk takers: individuals willing to challenge assumptions of accepted norms and values, new role models that help us see that it is possible to transcend old physical, intellectual, and emotional stereotypes, people willing to bring into action the necessary cultural transformation and give voice to the experience through their life stories.

The work of Carol Gilligan (1990) and Emily Hancock (1989) both identify a time in childhood when the girl challenges the voices of authority. In Hancock's book, *The Girl Within,* the state of being of young girls is more assured than challenged. It is as if the girl is so busy listening to the self and the universe she is engaged in exploring that she does not hear the voices of society that threaten her own voice. This early exploration of self is often interrupted and self awareness remains underdeveloped or not always fully regained. Feminists are now exploring what environments and opportunities need to exist for the self to be regained.

The voices of those experiencing disability as a part of their own whole and dynamic reality represent not so much the recovery of lost words as the emergence of words and voices that were silenced in past generations. For those of us whose experience of womanhood in America is shaped in contexts that somehow mark us as different or alien to those who surround us, the initial finding of voice may be a more solitary task. At least so it seems when I reflect back to what my own experience has been as a woman with a disability growing up in America of the fifties and sixties. So much of our presence was responded to with questions, doubts, and outright negation that affirmation was hard to come by.

We live at a time when the culture we are a part of is being challenged to embrace a broader range of diversity, to leave behind the melting pot to make room for the retention of ethnic identities, in an America of economic uncertainties and aging baby boomers. During this transition perhaps the journeys of women with disabilities can remind the larger culture of the diverse ways available for individuals to develop and understand our own humanity; to retain diversity through that understanding; to allow each person to plumb the depths and find our own voices, our own selfhood in a community of diversity.

Twenty five, even ten years ago, many who lived with severe disabilities would have died. Others with a broad range of physical, intellectual, or mental conditions were locked up as misfits or patients. Treated not as individuals but as aberrations from human norms; many were placed in institutions for medical or custodial care and received either rehabilitation or neglect or an odd mix of the two as professionals tried to fix what they often did not begin to understand. Many of us have grown up now and have a story to tell about what it feels like to grow up disabled in a world seeking certainties. Sadly it's still happening; we live in a society that has begun to see the limitations of institutionalizing those among us who grow old or have physical or mental disabilities: after all, one day many of us will have lived into old age and will be expected to go quietly into those bleak wards of institutional night to count our breaths till morning, because we are not quite ready to shed the skin we've outgrown. Instead of alternatives we have a vacuum and it is filled by homeless, institutionalized, and marginalized people, by bored and angry people in settings where they do not belong or that have not yet accepted and made room for their difference, their experience. The elderly and those of us with disabilities join other minorities who are being marginalized by a society moving into obsolescence, living out outmoded and outdated stereotypes. Our culture needs an explosion of creativity (economic, technological, social and interpersonal) if it is to stay kinetic and responsive enough to give expression to the diversity and the gifts its members contain.

These are new voices calling, cajoling, and singing to be heard. I am not at all sure that it is a different story, but perhaps it needs to be brought home differently as new cultures and technologies evolve, bringing forth new conflicts and new opportunities. People who were considered unreachable now speak with the aid of interpreters, facilitated communication, and technological aids. Teens dance and do ropes courses in wheelchairs, instead of buying into a label of dysfunctional. Men and women I know speak of their experiences with psychiatric disabilities as a journey to connectedness, a healing process mislabeled as illness.

But it is a struggle to be heard. It is a struggle to hear your own voice when the experience you bring to the world is not one that others share. These are journeys of connectedness and separation, of conflict and reconciliation, of isolation, affirmation, and despair. They are not isolated from the experience of difference as felt through gender, race, cultural difference or class; but they have new elements, new turnings on an old wheel. Over time those of us with similar experiences have learned to search for kindred voices so that we too gain the hearing that Carol Gilligan (1990) has so clearly identified as essential to trust, community, and intimacy.

I met with six women to discuss the impact of disability on their lives, their sense of self, their womanhood. Four of these women had disabilities; two were parents of daughters with disabilities; each had professional as well as personal experience with disability issues. Disability experiences varied; the women quoted in this article had dealt with mobility related disabilities or psychiatric disabilities, though I also talked with a woman who has a severe and progressive hearing loss. Her perspective influenced this article even though she is not quoted. The shape and content of the writing is influenced by my own experience with disability and by the many women with physical, sensory, cognitive, and mobility related disabilities I have known over the years. In the interviews, I wanted to explore how the human experience with disability had transformed their lives and affected their perspectives. I chose women I sensed had a story to tell; people born to struggle, make connections, women who seemed to be survivors. This was not random statistical research. I wanted to talk to people who were creating their own road maps.

Most of the women I spoke to saw themselves as rebels, either as a part of their character or because their individual gifts inadvertently challenged the status quo: young women whose athletic prowess and intellectual curiosity outstripped their brothers; women who opposed the Vietnam war during their college years; the girl who refused to lose herself in the role of patient in a family of medical professionals; and mothers who refused to accept the failure labels either for themselves as a parent or for their child who was born disabled. These woman by intent or accident were well suited to deal with the dichotomies presented by disability. They defined themselves as rebels, liked challenges, and liked to raise questions. The conflicts raised around disability were not always comfortable but they always raised necessary questions, inherent conflicts, issues that without the disability experiences might never have emerged.

Even a rebel may not be comfortable challenging the status quo without role models and peers, and may do so out of necessity, not choice. That is when an instinctive inclination for rebellion comes in handy. Lee and Peggy raised their children in the sixties and were part of a first generation of parents of children with severe disabilities who chose to raise them at home rather than sending them to institutions. For both of them and for their children the role models and support groups existed somewhere in the future, waiting somewhere to be created along with Head Start programs and local theater groups. Sometimes they were criticized by professionals who felt that their decision to raise severely disabled children at home went against the best interest of the disabled child and the family as a whole.

It was rare then for a mother to align herself with adults with disabilities, to imagine her severely disabled child as a person who would one day grow to adulthood and want to live independently. As Peggy said:

I know that what I wanted for Lisa, was for her as an adult to have her own life and for her to be around people, adults with disabilities, who could speak for themselves . . . there are some things I just realize need to happen because the most important thing is for a person to feel they have some self worth . . . Maybe [because of] my struggle internally . . . the fact that I grew up not knowing any self worth . . . perhaps my pain was also my gift to my children. . .

And when I look back and think of what we did and what beautiful people my daughter was able to connect with . . . you see, because I believe that we can't be everything to every-body; if you surround yourself with people that you expect the best of, maybe I have that belief inside, that they can see different models. It is the most important part of education . . . to surround yourself with different people . . . the kids get the best of what a community has to offer. . . . somewhere inside I just trust that education isn't really in the schools. It just basi-cally, bottom line, is really that we meet a lot of people and see how they live their lives.

For women with disabilities the role models out there to meet in order to see how they live their lives are just beginning to emerge. I grew up needing to be my own role model in the same way that each morning when I sat up and put my feet on the floor of the bedroom I had to slowly rise and find my balance, moving across the floor with my arms out until I found my center and got oriented again to being in the body and moving through the world on my awkward legs. Ann who I interviewed said that her first role model was an older disability rights activist she finally met when she was in her twenties. She had a friend with disabilities before then, but not a role model, the opportunity to see someone integrating dis-ability into a strong self image. She had gone through her childhood and into college wanting to deny the part of her that was disabled, ('hating the lower half of my body,' as she put it); had been drawn to black studies and had thought the first disability rights activist she met were pretty bizarre for even considering disability a rights issue or a cultural concern.

Living one's life with a disability means kicking aside what Ann terms "ablisms." It means taking risks not just for the sake of challenging assumptions but in order to live an individual life. I'm glad that I've raised a kid and learned the value of massage, relaxation and fun so that I can say to other women with disabilities, "Yes; it's possible to raise a kid (and have a wonderful time doing it). Yes, it makes sense your legs (or arms, or brain) are tired; and no, walking more is not what you need: maybe you should get a good leg rub and back massage."

I'm glad–more than glad–that I've been able to have my own life, raise a kid, write poems and songs, find a sweetheart after years of living alone, speak in public, be alone, garden, ache, listen to other people's stories and take risks, because without risks there is no opportunity to experience a life that takes you beyond your original expectations. Ann and I talk about this: the importance of risk and the importance of day to day opportunities for happiness. Take away risk and how much opportunity for self determination is left? Diana's cerebral palsy makes her hands so jittery she can't hold ski poles, so she skies down Mount Ascutney (in Vermont) without poles. It's called creative problem solving, and it's not without risk. But Diana (whose braver than I am) would be the first to tell you it's fun.

She and I and all the women with disabilities I spoke to either had gone through or are still trying to deal with questions of body image and cultural expectations (but then, so are probably all the women we know). We live in a culture hung up on physical attributes and physical acceptance. One reason both aging and disability is hard for us to deal with is because they both require acceptance of realities and images our culture tries to overlook; but wrinkles and size and limps are just a few of the attributes our society questions. One young woman spoke of how hard it felt believing that the first man she loved didn't accept her because of her disability; and how liberating it was to find out later that her disability had nothing to do with it: he is gay and they are still good friends.

Our society is rather parochial and seems to cope with difference poorly: we want to integrate it, manage it, do something about it; anything but accept it. So we end up with special education instead of an education that integrates all learners. We end up with racial ghettos, minority movements, a covert class structure all because we have yet to learn how to create communities that allow for and embrace diversity.

Because so much of the women's movement in this country is based on pretty stereotypical assumptions, some of the issues other women fight about, and for, represent cultural norms (however limiting or faulty) that we are not viewed through or included in.

For example, not all of us take being a sex object for granted. For someone who does not expect to be viewed as attractive, a wolf whistle from a passing truck can be a great experience. On the other hand many men, with disabilities and without, may compound sexist attitudes when thinking about or relating to women with disability. We are sometimes treated not as individuals, but as many of the stereotypes of women's sexuality come to life; and when our disabilities cause mobility or communication problems, we may also be subjected to being objectified and subjected to unwanted attentions due to the effects of our disabilities. I still remember the French teacher who lived in the town in which I grew up who seemed to think that my cooking ability and my disability went hand in hand with my being a potentially good wife for some man who wouldn't have to worry about me being too fast for him . . . (to use a loaded phrase).

Not all of us take jobs for granted either. Equality of opportunity has to come before equality of pay. Like Black women, women with disabilities are ranked far below White able-bodied men and women when it comes to career options and salary levels. Poverty or the fear of it is something we know about (Asch & Fine, 1984).

The feminization of poverty and the gender bias in our culture compound the unique issues relating to disability so that you have a double whammy of discrimination and stereotypes to deal with. The advantage being that women have been raised to expect discrimination; men with disabilities and without the experience of color bias or other minority identification are poorly prepared to challenge stereotypes. Yet men with disabilities must be willing to challenge stereotypes if they hope to find self esteem.

Growing up and dealing with hidden as well as the more visible aspects of disability, I often felt alien in the homes of my parents and our neighbors, as though I faced people from different cultures across the dinner table and the living room floor. My brothers and sisters didn't give me that feeling but almost everyone else did. I felt that if I was going to find myself and survive, I had to find ways to transcribe my life into a language that had no words for part of what my daily experience was. The women's movement only now is dealing with our issues and not always doing it well.

Such little actions challenge the status quo. A woman in Boston wears sneakers to work and gains the admiration of her nondisabled peers. She says:

> A couple of months ago I realized that my body was responsible for giving me my politics . . . how if I didn't have cerebral palsy I wouldn't have the politics I've developed. Also, I don't dress to project myself as a good looking person . . . I dress how I want to dress, and that means being an individual and not wanting to buy into 'the way women should dress,' or it doesn't matter how people are going to look at me anyhow so I might just as well be comfortable.

> I think all women struggle; we're told so often . . . I mean, just the phrase, the words, 'make up' itself says: You're not good enough. Every morning you need to make up . . . 'make up' . . . look different in order to be socially acceptable. That's wrong . . . and I find it . . . really silly.

We talked, laughing about the dangers of shaving your legs if you have involuntary movements. She said,

> I think having a disability and not being about to shave my legs; because if I did . . . I'd never have made it . . . I would be a mess. If I tried to put on mascara, I'd put my eye out, you know; I could never physically do it. When I was a teenager it used to bother me; but now you know it doesn't.

> It's interesting; I never thought of it this way, but it's true that I've had the experience that because I'm disabled I can't do certain things that other people do because that's what you're 'supposed to do'; like sports, or dressing up, walking a certain way, or wearing heels and other things relating to careers . . . and I can't do certain things. The experience of disability

allows us to think . . . like I have to think of my body. I can't keep working overtime, all the time; even though I can work for a long time. I have to give myself breaks . . . but having come to terms with that part of myself, it's meant that I'm dealing with having a better balance in life as a person, not just as a person with a disability. So I think that we're able to be who we are as women 'cause we don't fit into the stereotype maybe.

This is perhaps one of the more central messages that disability experience has to give the larger culture. We need to find ways to help people recognize and follow their own pole star. Kay speaks of this in her own experiences with mental illness: The doctor who helped her the most was the one who expected her to help herself. The ways she speaks of it, the kinetic quality of the relationship makes the human connection happen. As Kay put it:

I was laying in bed, I was fat, wouldn't brush my teeth, wouldn't comb my hair, also having major headaches at the time. Finally my psychologist comes in, a Ph.D. . . . he was the one bright spot in my life, he was very good looking . . . he had lots of positive energy. I wouldn't say I had a crush on him . . . although most of his female patients probably did . . . I had a crush on his energy.

He was very helpful to me in my process of getting well, if you will . . . but he came in one day, and he plopped himself down (with all this energy) and he had his hands on his legs; he would be right where I was: he didn't mind telling me a joke now and then. He said, 'I'll tell you what. I've been coming here for days and I don't see you doing anything, and I'm not going to waste my time. There are lots of other people who want to see me and want to get better. I'm going to come back in three days and see what your decision is; if you're not willing to help yourself, I'm bailing out of this mess.'

I just went . . . my mouth went down to the floor; and that's what my turning point was . . . for my recovery if you will . . . though I'm not sure it was an illness . . . but whatever . . . For me turning my life around for myself. Because before that I didn't have any sense of [who I was]. That little five year old had a clear sense and then it got lost in the shuffle . . . and everything became external . . . all those doctors, this medication and the hospital . . . and none of it doing any good and I realized that I had to do good for myself; whether it's mental illness, whether it's caused by whatever I've been through, whatever I've done, doesn't matter. I have to somehow take control of that. I have to be responsible and let the medications . . . I was on them for nine years, they're only tools, that I can use, and I have to make them work, or not, or nothing's going to work. In just that short session, I got up and I took a shower and I panted and puffed and almost fainted; I was heavy. I was in the hospital seventeen days and lost seventeen pounds. I lost the weight myself and I kept it off. I have a very strong core, that goes back to my younger girl, the stronger Kay, I really have depended on her to keep me going in life. Others say people have to have a support group to make it but the hardest things I've struggled with I've done by reaching down into my core.

Telling this story Kay talked about the time in her life just prior to the incident when she was having a harder and harder time coping. She spent a long time each morning having to put her mask on every day before she went to work. The make up again; to hide the nonacceptable self.

Living with disabilities–whether they be physical, mental or cognitive–demands such an array of responses that it is impossible to face your self without dealing with the disability that is part of one's unique human experience. It begins to transform your sense of each segment of the lifespan; it subtlety influences your experience of your body, your sense of self, your place in the world around you. It both points out and challenges limitations. For many of us our struggle for common ground and kindred understanding is not found in the women's movement but in the struggles of racial minorities and the poor. It is hard for girls and young women to see disability pride as something worth having; too many attitudes and stereotypes pervade the way we are treated, the way we perceive our own bodies when we accept our body through the eyes and assumptions of the ablebodied. To take up our own vision and acknowledge our own experience is often a lonely task, difficult to come to.

As my friend Ann put it:

> I think we are the only group of people who are trying to push that broadening of acceptance beyond culture and race, toward a broadening acceptance for everybody . . . that would free men and women from the stereotypes of how men and women need to be emotionally or physically . . . You know what I mean: I think we have the potential for questioning the culture and moving it into another direction . . . I think we're a very positive force in that sense. If we don't push the culture into having the physical and emotional diversity, medical technology is going to be used to rehabilitate us all onto a very rigid ground where everyone is going to get fixed, redone, whatever; you know, a white, blond, blue-eyed, perfect body image. As medical technology progresses, there is the tendency to use it for a pure fix and get us to conform to those stereotypes that men and women are struggling with in the culture. So just as technology is allowing people with disabilities to live longer and be more independent, the technology may also work against us if we're not careful. In trying to use technology to eliminate disability that also prevents human diversity and what we have as a race to learn from our own diversity. I think we need to resist that tendency in order to push the culture to having that physical and emotional diversity.

Ann went on to say that she wanted the culture to move to an acceptance of human life that was not so constrained by images and expectations of people limited by or locked into their physical bodies. One reason I feel so certain that the disability rights movement requires a transformation of culture is because the lessons I and others have learned through our individual and shared experience with disability stir up such fundamental conflicts (with the status quo and the myths and stereotypes about being human that our culture embraces), that our experiences cannot be voiced without changing the personal and social perspectives of those people able to hear what these experiences say about what it is to be human.

When I speak to audiences about disability rights and the awareness it requires, I tell them that we are remaking the cultures we live in and redefining what it is to be human. Individuals who would have died or been forced to live in institutions are now living to remake the meanings of disability, aging, and human potential. We are joined by others of different races and cultures whose perceptions, histories, and cultural identities are transforming America. Let's get on with it.

I believe the perspective Ann and others embrace speaks to a way of living that Bettina Aptheker (1989) referred to when she noted, "that the dailiness of women's lives structures a different way of knowing and a different way of thinking" (pp. 253-254).

This way of being may be feminist, but it goes beyond feminism. It speaks to what it is to be human. As she put it:

> The process that comes from this way of knowing has to be at the center of a women's scholarship. This is why I have been drawn to the poetry and to the stories: because they are layered, because more than one truth is represented, because there is ambiguity and paradox. When we work together in coalitions, or on the job, or in academic settings, or in the community, we have to allow for this ambiguity and paradox, respect each other, our cultures, our integrity, our dignity. (pp. 253-254)

Bettina Aptheker's (1989) thoughts about the structure of women's lives representing a new structure, a more prism-like paradigm reminds me of one of the more striking allusions two women independently chose to use about their experiences with disability: life as a puzzle. Lee, the mother of a disability rights activist and one herself, used the image when I asked her what her love of art and theater had in common with the work she does in disability politics. She chose the image of puzzles to express their commonality. She spoke of both activities requiring the creation of expressions that spoke to cultural needs. And when Ann spoke of her involvement in adaptive recreation she spoke of the joy she experiences in puzzling out ways of interacting with a rocky cliff, a ropes course, or wheelchair races as solving a puzzle; finding, creating new ways to interact with the environment in a body that does not behave in the predictable and understandable ways of a human with no spinal cord injury. She also spoke eloquently of the art of climbing out of her wheelchair and feeling her way down a rocky slope to water as a way of communicating with the stones through touch. It makes perfect sense that problem solving and art occur together as we seek honest ways to live out our women's sense of being; makes perfect sense that coming to terms with age and disability takes on the tonal quality of jazz, a kind of free fall into composition, a note by note inquiry into life.

This kind of inquiry and openness requires a great deal of us, and also challenges our academic, political, social, and therapeutic institutions. We speak of nothing less than a different way of living into the future; moving beyond the constructs and constraints of old cultural and gender "isms." For those of us dealing personally with ageing or with disability or other minority experiences that the culture is not always able to understand and honor, the approach to life which I speak of is paramount to survival, expression, recognition, and joy. But as Bettina Aptheker (1989) recognized, the institutions, even those "isms" and systems that pride themselves for their radical spirit, often close the door on the new voice that seeks to speak to them:

> As we have pressured against racial and sex discrimination, institutional doors have opened, however tenuously and with whatever reluctance. Some of us have been allowed in, but nothing about the values of those institutions or their rules of success have changed, whether they be academic, corporate, ecclesiastic, political, medical or juridical. The point is to change the values and the rules and to change the process by which they are established and enforced. The point is to integrate ideas about love and healing, about balance and connection, about beauty and growing into our everyday way of being. We have to believe in the value of our ways of knowing, our ways of doing things. (p. 254)

REFERENCES

Aptheker, B. (1989). *Tapestries of life*. Amherst, MA: The University of Massachusetts Press, (pp. 253-254).

Asch, A., & Fine, M. (1984). *Women with disabilities*. Philadelphia, PA: Temple University Press.

Gilligan, C. (1990). Teaching Shakespeare's sister: Notes from the underground of female adolescence. In Gilligan C., Lyons N. & Hanmer T.J., (Eds.), *Making Connections: The relational worlds of adolescent girls at Emma Willard School*, (p. 27). Cambridge, MA: Harvard Univ. Press.

Hancock, L. (1989). *The girl within*. New York, NY: Dutton.

SURVIVING SALEM
with a movement disorder
and several witches' tits

Patricia Ranzoni

The Samuel Parris preachers
are still fooling the faithful
from behind Bible proof: "I name
my text." Still condemning,
condoning, by ego, design,
however divinely inspired. Still
rending families, towns, from behind
belief to control, play, manipulate, steal;
deciding good, evil, on their terms.
Seeing Satan where they want to,
witches where they choose. Sentencing
to guilt in the name of fear. Thank God
for more Sarahs daring to defy
our need for devils. Lord knows
I'd have swung from the hanging tree.

[Haworth co-indexing entry note]: "SURVIVING SALEM with a movement disorder and several witches' tits." Ranzoni, Patricia. Co-published simultaneously in *Women & Therapy* (The Haworth Press, Inc.) Vol. 14, No. 3/4, 1993, p. 211; and: *Women with Disabilities: Found Voices* (ed: Mary E. Willmuth, and Lillian Holcomb) The Haworth Press, Inc., 1993, p. 211. Multiple copies of this article/chapter may be purchased from The Haworth Document Delivery Center [1-800-3-HAWORTH; 9:00 a.m. - 5:00 p.m. (EST)].

DATE DUE
